SLEEP AND DREAMS

SLEEP AND DREAMS

Dr. Alvin Silverstein and Virginia B. Silverstein

J. B. LIPPINCOTT COMPANY/PHILADELPHIA AND NEW YORK

U. S. Library of Congress Cataloging in Publication Data

Silverstein, Alvin.
  Sleep and dreams.

  SUMMARY: Examines what is known and being learned through research about
that one third of the human life that is spent sleeping and dreaming.
  1. Sleep—Juvenile literature. 2. Dreams—Juvenile literature. [1. Sleep. 2.
Dreams]   I. Silverstein, Virginia B., joint author. II. Title.
QP425.S588   612.821   73-13825
ISBN-0-397-31325-X

For D. S. B.
who gave us our start

CONTENTS

ONE   The Mysterious Third of Life   13

TWO   The Clocks Within   19

THREE   Sleep in the Animal World   33

FOUR   A Night's Sleep   53

FIVE   The Land of Dreams   69

SIX   What Makes Us Sleep   95

SEVEN   Without Sleep   105

EIGHT   Remedies for Troubled Sleep   117

NINE   How To Get a Good Night's Sleep   129

TEN   The Long Sleeps   134

ELEVEN   The Future of Sleep Research   148

           Index   154

SLEEP AND DREAMS

ONE
The Mysterious Third of Life

We all must sleep. From the time before birth, through the long years of our life, to the very day that we die, a rhythm of sleep and wakefulness goes endlessly on. Indeed, we spend more time sleeping than in any other activity. We spend an average of more than twenty years of our lives in a strange state of what seems like almost complete withdrawal from the world.

Some primitive people believe that the soul actually leaves the body during sleep and wanders about. They think that one must be very careful not to wake a sleeper suddenly, but instead should do so slowly and gently, to give the wandering soul a chance to return.

But the time we spend asleep is not really disconnected from our lives. We all know that during sleep we gain the rest and refreshment that permits us to carry on during the following day. Most of the critical activities of life continue. We breathe on steadily. The heart beats methodically, pumping blood throughout the body and thus providing the trillions of cells with fresh nutrients. Each of these cells continues to function, maintaining its own life and cooperating with other cells in the harmoniously integrated systems of the body.

The sleeper is not really cut off from the outside world. Although his eyes are closed, many of his senses are still alert. Sounds are picked up by the ears and are filtered through the brain. The sleeper's brain may ignore sounds that it does not consider important. But certain sounds may bring an almost instant awakening. The loud ring of an alarm clock or a telephone may shatter sleep. The mother of a newborn baby may sleep soundly through a violent thunderstorm, only to awaken immediately at the faint whimpering of her child.

While sleeping, a person may snore, turn about, or even walk; he may mumble, talk, or cry out. Stray thoughts drift in and out of his mind, and may be woven into the fanciful stories and scenes that we call dreams.

Not all people sleep in the same way. An infant may sleep for fourteen to eighteen hours a day. He sleeps and wakes, sleeps and wakes again. Gradually he begins to merge two or three short naps into one long sleep, and adapts to the family's schedule. His need for sleep gradually decreases as he grows older until, as an adult, he sleeps about eight hours each day. Yet even adults may have quite different sleep patterns. One person may need nine hours of sleep a day, while another can get along quite well on seven. The great inventor Thomas Alva Edison liked to boast that he needed only four or five hours of sleep a day. But in addition to his sleep at night, he would curl up in a chair for short naps during the day. Many other people, from prizefighters to presidents, have found that short naps in the daytime can refresh them and give them new energy for their activities. But some people do not have the ability to nap during the day at all, or awaken from a nap groggy and disoriented.

People also have quite varied attitudes toward sleep. A young baby will usually go quite readily to bed, calmly accepting the

People all need sleep and must get it wherever they can, whether in a child's comfortable bed at home or on a hard bench in a bus station.

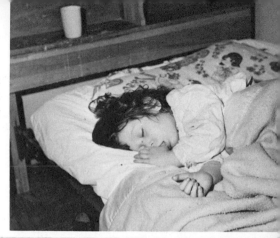

sleep that his body needs. But as he grows more independent, he may begin to fight sleep, waging a series of delaying actions and even throwing tantrums, although he may be cranky and drooping from fatigue. Often a nightly ritual develops, with a story, a good-night kiss, a drink of water and an extra trip to the bathroom, and perhaps a series of questions such as, "Is it going to be lightning and thunder tonight?"—anything to put off the moment when the light must at last go out.

Eventually most people grow to accept the need for sleep, and even to welcome it as an escape from boredom or from problems of the outside world. Yet often bedtime comes as an annoying interruption to interesting activities, and many people share Edison's feeling that sleep is a waste of time, and if only one had enough willpower, the need for much of it could be overcome.

Some people have tried to do without sleep, either for a night or two in emergencies or for longer periods in experiments. These attempts have revealed how important sleep is to normal life. Sleep-deprived people quickly become irritable, and their reactions begin to slow down. They find it more and more difficult to stay awake; eventually they may fall into a light sleep for seconds at a time while they are standing or even walking.

Considering the importance of sleep and the amount of time we spend on it, it is surprising how little we really know about this mysterious third of our lives. Modern sleep research began in the 1930s, with the work of Dr. Nathaniel Kleitman at the University of Chicago. Studying the sleep patterns of infants and the effects on adults who are kept awake, Dr. Kleitman gradually became convinced that sleep and wakefulness are two parts of a single process, a cycle that repeats itself again and again, like the ebb and flow of the tides.

Dr. Kleitman has been joined by many other sleep researchers, working in a number of laboratories all over the world. Modern sleep researchers use a sophisticated array of instruments in their work. Electrodes taped to the heads of volunteer sleepers pick up minute pulses of electricity from the brain. As these brain waves are recorded, other pickups record the movements of the sleeper's eyes. The breathing rate, the heartbeat, the muscle tension, and the secretions of various glands may also be monitored. From time to time, the investigators may wake the subject and ask him if he was dreaming. His replies are recorded on tape and then correlated with the electroencephalogram (EEG), the brain-wave tracing. As the night goes on, the volunteer sleeps peacefully, un-

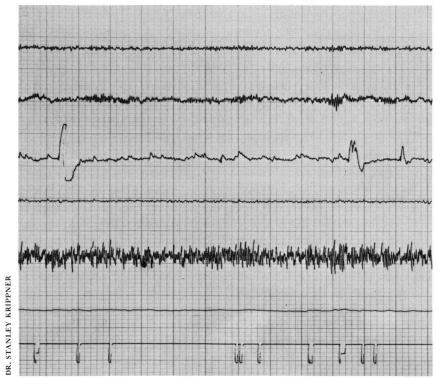

A small section of an electroencephalogram tracing made at Maimonides Medical Center, Brooklyn, New York.

mindful of the dangling wires that surround him. Meanwhile, the weary researchers fight to stay awake as they continually check their apparatus and watch for any interesting changes in the sleeper.

The space flights of the astronauts who have circled the earth and traveled to the moon and back focused the attention of the world on the problems of sleep. Miniaturized instruments radioed back information on the depth, nature, and length of the astronauts' sleep. Much valuable information on sleep in zero gravity and in the isolation of space was gathered.

Our knowledge of sleep is growing as a result of information flowing out of hundreds of laboratories throughout the world. More and more we are learning that for many organisms sleep is a fundamental process deeply involved in the basic rhythms of life.

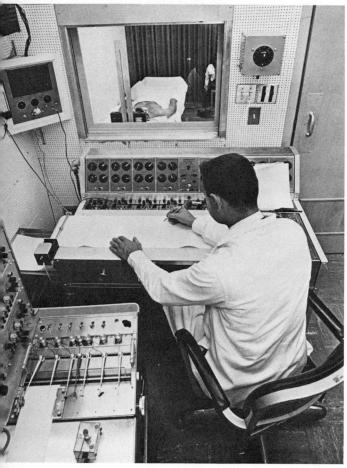

A research worker checks his instruments at a sleep laboratory at the University of Florida.

DR. WILSE WEBB

TWO
The Clocks Within

For billions of years the earth has revolved around the sun, turning on its axis as it hurtles through space. From the very beginning, when life first appeared on our world, it has been exposed to an endless procession of seasons and alternating periods of light and darkness.

From the very beginning of life on earth, there has been a constant struggle for survival among its varied forms. Any advantage that an organism could gain in the fight for life would help it to live to produce more of its kind and thus promote the survival of its species. These advantages came from adaptations to various conditions of the environment. Some organisms developed the ability to bind the energy into chemical compounds that could be stored as food materials. From these ancient organisms came the modern green plants. Some organisms became able to live outside of the waters that had been the homes of their ancestors. Soon the barren lands of the earth were covered with animals and plants.

The creatures of the water and land found many advantages in adapting to the rhythms of our planet—the ceaseless ebb and flow of the tides, the changing seasons, the alternation of night and day.

The leaves of many plants pass through a cycle of movements that seems to be timed to the hours of the day and night. Peas and beans raise their leaves during the day and lower them at night. The petals of day lily flowers open during the day and fold up tight at night. Within the plants, the rates of certain chemical reactions also rise and fall according to cycles lasting about twenty-four hours. Certain reactions of photosynthesis occur only in sunlight, while growth is fastest at night.

Animals, too, have daily cycles of activity. Most rodents, such predators as owls and cats, and such insects as cockroaches and

The owl is perhaps most often thought of as the typical nocturnal animal. Its eyes are adapted for seeing in partial darkness, and its fluffy feathers make its flight almost noiseless.

Photo by BUHNNE

moths are nocturnal: they are most active at night and rest for most of the daylight hours. Other animals—most songbirds; bees and butterflies; grazing animals such as horses, cows, antelopes, and giraffes; and also man and his closest relatives, the monkeys —are diurnal creatures: the daylight hours are their active time, and they retire to some quiet shelter to rest or sleep at night. The rhythms of their bodies—the rise and fall of the body temperature, the flow of various chemicals through the blood and their excretion with the urine—are also timed to these daily cycles of activity.

Such rhythms, which are repeated regularly at periods of about twenty-four hours, are called circadian rhythms, from Latin words meaning "about a day."

Many processes within our bodies are timed to a cycle of about twenty-four hours. If the body temperature is taken every hour or so throughout the day or night, and the values are plotted on a graph, each person is found to have a characteristic pattern. The temperature rises and falls about two degrees every twenty-four hours. Some people's temperature curves rise very rapidly after awakening and then begin to fall in the afternoon and evening. For others the curve rises very slowly at first, reaches a peak in the late afternoon or evening, and does not begin to drop until quite late in the day. In all cases the temperature curve is at its lowest during the time of sleep. People tend to feel most wide-awake and can work most efficiently at the high point of their temperature. You may have noticed that some people bounce out of bed bright and early and are cheerful and active during the early part of the day, then grow tired in the evening and go to bed quite early. Others find it difficult to get up in the morning and do not seem able to get going very well until afternoon; during the evening, they are wide-awake and hate to go to bed.

Our world, with its nine-to-five workday and early schoolday, seems to be designed for the "early people." Many of those who are most efficient in the evenings tend to feel out of step, unless they can find a school or job with a late shift, or work that they can do at home on their own schedule. People can usually adapt to a different schedule if necessary, but it seems to be more difficult for some people than for others.

Together with the temperature cycle, other processes in the body are also timed to a cycle of about twenty-four hours. The glands secrete their hormones, the cells of the body divide, and the kidneys, heart, and other organs work in tune with circadian rhythms. All these rhythms can gradually be adjusted when we travel to a new time zone or change to a different work shift. But just how fixed is the twenty-four-hour period? Can that, too, be changed?

This question is becoming more and more important as submarines stay under the seas for months at a time and astronauts venture out into space. Away from the control of the earth's day and night, man could work out new patterns of working and sleeping, if his inner clocks will let him. Several experiments have already been conducted to find out how much the rhythms of our lives can be changed.

In 1938 sleep researcher Nathaniel Kleitman and one of his students went down into Mammoth Cave, Kentucky, to live for a time. The temperature was unchanging, and they could set the periods of "night" and "day" according to the times they turned their electric lights off and on. First they tried to live on a twenty-one-hour day. They were able to adapt fairly well and lived this way for a month. Then they tried stretching their day to twenty-eight hours. The student was able to adapt, but Dr. Kleitman found that he could not. His body kept to its normal twenty-four-hour cycles, and he felt ill and irritable.

In another experiment, groups of students from the London Medical Research Council traveled to Spitsbergen, Norway, where the daylight lasts all summer long. The students were given "cheating" wristwatches, which looked normal but were set to run fast or slow, so that some of the students were really living

Life on a nuclear submarine, which often means staying underwater for long periods of time, has made it apparent that man can adapt his cycles to conform to a new and different environment. These bunks are individually lighted and air conditioned.

on twenty-one-hour days, while others were living on twenty-eight-hour days. Some of the students were unable to adapt to the new schedules, but some did begin to show a twenty-one-hour or twenty-eight-hour temperature cycle. Samples of the students' urine were taken and tested for various chemicals to see how well the different systems of the body had adapted to the different day lengths. Among the students who had adapted best, some substances in the urine showed new patterns that matched the changed temperature cycles. But other substances did not—they still varied regularly every twenty-four hours. The different chemical reactions of the body were now out of phase with each other, which meant that the systems of the body were no longer working properly.

The lives of other organisms on our planet are also timed to a variety of rhythms: the ebb and flow of the tides, the lunar month, governed by the movement of the moon about the earth, and the seasons of the year. Indeed, much of the information on patterns of sleep and activity is being gathered through observations and experiments on plants and animals.

Some of the animals that live at the edge of the sea come out to feed when the waters of the high tide wash over them. Oysters, clams, and barnacles are most active at this time. As the tide recedes, the barnacles retreat into their shells, and clams dig themselves into the soft sand until the waters return. Other seashore dwellers, such as shore birds and fiddler crabs, come out to feed at low tide, when the sand at the edge of the sea is exposed. Not only do a fiddler crab's activities follow a cycle matched to the tides, but the color of its body changes according to the time of day. During the day it darkens, while at night it becomes pale.

The mating cycles of many animals are timed to the phases of the moon. In the spring, along the coast of California near Los Angeles, small silvery fish called grunions come in to lay their eggs in the sand. Their visits always fall just after the full moon, when the tides are the highest of the lunar month. The lapping ocean waters will not reach so high again until two weeks later, when the eggs are hatching and the tiny fish are ready to be carried out again to sea.

In the waters of the West Indies, marine worms called fire worms, which live in burrows at the bottom of the sea, come to the top of the water to mate. The females, whose bodies give off a glowing light, swim up first. They are followed by the males, each of which has two small flashing headlights. Swimming in tight circles together, the worms shed their eggs and sperm into the water, then dive back down to their burrows. These strange courtship swims occur quite regularly each month during the summer, just two days after the full moon.

Even the timing of the human menstrual cycle is very close to the length of the lunar month. Although the menstrual cycle is not coordinated with any particular phase of the moon, and indeed varies widely among different women, scientists believe that this rhythm, too, may once have been governed by the cycle of changing forces between earth and moon.

The changing seasons help to govern the lives of plants and of many animals. Many plants will not flower until a certain time of year, no matter when they were planted and how large they are when their flowering time has come. Researchers have found that these plants are very sensitive to the lengths of the periods of daylight and darkness. Similar cues, based on the length of night and day, seem to trigger the urge of migrating birds to fly north or south. Other animals, from frogs to bears, seem to sense the approaching cold of winter and retire to a long period of dormancy or hibernation.

Many of these biological clocks and calendars might seem to be easily explainable as responses to the changing conditions of the environment. But when scientists began to study these natural rhythms in the laboratory, they turned out to be far more complicated than had been suspected.

Bean plants grown in the laboratory still raise and lower their leaves in a twenty-four-hour rhythm, even when they are kept in total darkness. Fiddler crabs in a motionless tank of seawater in a darkened laboratory room continue to move about and rest and periodically change color in tune with the tides that no longer wash over them and the sun that they cannot see.

The noted zoologist Colin S. Pittendrigh, working at Princeton University, and various other researchers have conducted a number of experiments of this kind and found that the circadian rhythms do not seem to be disturbed when organisms are placed under conditions of constant light or constant darkness. Gradually it came to be believed that there is some sort of inner clock in living things, which is relatively independent of the environment. Yet the nature of this clock remained a mystery, and many facets of how it works seemed puzzling. For example, nearly all the chemical reactions within the body are quite sensitive to the temperature, speeding up as the temperature rises. Yet the biological clocks remained constant over a wide range of temperatures.

The idea of independent inner clocks seemed to be supported by some interesting experiments on the navigating abilities of birds and insects. The pioneer of bee research, Karl von Frisch, discovered that when honeybee scouts discover a rich source of food, they fly back and report to the other bees in the hive. He observed specially marked bees under red light (bees are blind to red light, and so behaved as though they were in their normal darkness inside the hive). Gradually von Frisch unraveled the code of the bee dances, in which the scout bee moves about on the wall of the hive in a circle or a figure eight, and gives the surrounding worker bees information on the location of the food. In her run up the middle of the figure eight, the scout wags her abdomen back and forth, and the rate of wagging gives the distance from the hive to the food. The slant of the dance figure on the wall of the hive gives the direction in which the worker bees must fly to reach the food, plotting their flight by the angle to the position of the sun. Even though the position of the sun in the sky changes as the day goes on, the bees still can find their way to the food. In fact, if the bees are kept inside the hive for several hours after the "waggle dance," they automatically adjust their flight pattern to the new position of the sun. Apparently they can consult a sort of inner clock and match it to the movement of the sun across the sky.

Curious about this inner clock, von Frisch conducted another experiment to find out how constant it is and whether it depends on factors in the environment. Working in Paris, he trained a group of bees to come for food (a dish of sugar water) at a certain hour every day. Then he had the bees flown to New York. If they were telling time by the position of the sun or other outside clues, the bees would have gone out for food at the proper hour, New York time. But instead, it was found that the bees were still keeping Paris time: they arrived at the feeding dish exactly twenty-four hours after their last feeding in Paris.

Yet biological clocks cannot be entirely independent, for they can be reset. After von Frisch's bees had been in New York for a while, they gradually changed over to New York time. Another zoologist, Frank A. Brown, Jr., of Northwestern University, obtained a similar result with a quite different organism. He col-

World-wide time zones—the international date line is in the middle of the Pacific Ocean. When it's 3 A.M. in San Francisco, it's 11 A.M. in London.

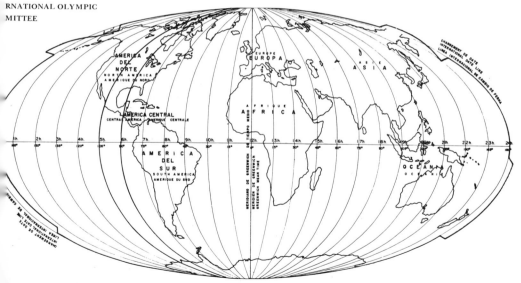

lected oysters on the beaches of New Haven, Connecticut, and brought them back to his laboratory in Evanston, Illinois, almost 800 miles west. As he had expected, when he placed the oysters in pans of seawater in a darkroom, they continued to open their shells at their normal feeding time, when high tides washed over the Connecticut coast. But then, within about two weeks, the oysters adjusted to their new location. They began to open and close their shells according to the position of the moon over Evanston, corresponding to what would have been high and low tides there, if this midwestern city had a seacoast.

Biological clocks in a variety of organisms can be reset fairly readily. One researcher, W. C. Young, wanted to study the mating behavior of guinea pigs. The guinea pig female has a regular sexual cycle, and is willing to mate only at a certain point in the cycle—and this point always occurs in the middle of the night and the wee hours of the morning. This is a convenient hour for guinea pigs, which are nocturnal animals, but it is rather trying for human researchers to have to come to the laboratory in the middle of the night to watch them. Dr. Young solved the problem neatly by resetting his guinea pigs' inner clocks. He placed them in a windowless room and turned the lights on at night and off during the day. After a few weeks, the rodents had adjusted to the artificial day and night schedule, and they were active at a more convenient time for the scientists trying to study them.

What are the factors that control the inner clocks of living organisms, and help to set and reset them? The cycles of light and darkness seem to be controlling factors in many cases. It is believed that animals and plants may also be sensitive to other forces of the environment, such as the atmospheric pressure, the gravitational pull between earth and moon, and the earth's magnetic field. After his work with marine animals, Frank A. Brown, Jr., turned to other organisms. In one series of experiments, he sealed plugs from potato tubers in a respirometer, an instrument that measured their "breathing" rate, the amount of oxygen they took in. He found that this rate goes through daily cycles, which depend on changes in the atmospheric pressure. This was so even though the containers were tightly sealed, and the potato plugs were not in contact with the atmosphere. The potatoes acted like "living barometers," and even could be used to predict storms and other major changes in the weather.

In experiments on other organisms, it has been found that the biological clocks respond to changes in the earth's magnetic field and to radiations, such as the cosmic radiations that come from outer space.

What will be the effects of space travel on the inner clocks of living organisms? Can their natural rhythms still keep pace out of sight of the sun, outside the reach of the earth's gravity and its magnetic fields? Today's scientists are eager to find out. For humans have their own regular rhythms and cycles of living, and if these cycles become upset during long space missions, the lives of the astronauts might be in danger. Plans are being made to send up potatoes and other biological samples on satellites equipped with special instruments to measure their breathing rate and other rhythmic activities, to see whether the rhythms of life can indeed be maintained away from the familiar conditions of the earth.

The inner clocks of man himself are being studied more and more, as scientists are growing to realize how important they may be in our daily activities. As increasing numbers of people have begun to fly frequently in fast jets for long distances, cases of jet exhaustion have been noted. Lowell Thomas, a radio and television commentator and writer, was one of these frequent travelers. In one period of about a year, he flew on a number of trips to various parts of the world, crossing all twenty-four time zones at least twice. His schedule was so busy that he had very little time to rest between trips. After awhile, he began to feel ill. Several times he had alarming blackouts, in which he actually lost consciousness for brief periods. Then one day, after a jet flight half-

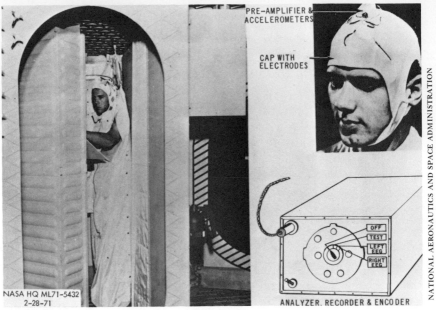

PRE-AMPLIFIER &
ACCELEROMETERS

CAP WITH
ELECTRODES

OFF
TEST
LEFT
EEG
RIGHT
EEG

NASA HQ ML71-5432
2-28-71

ANALYZER. RECORDER & ENCODER

Astronauts on Skylab are the subjects of experiments designed to find out how well man can sleep and adjust his rhythms outside the earth's gravitational field.

way around the world, he had a frightening attack. His hands began to shake, and he found it difficult to speak or move. He felt as though there were a thick sheet of glass separating him from the people around him. The doctor that Lowell Thomas called told him that he was suffering from jet exhaustion—he had traveled so much and lived on so many different time schedules that his biological clocks were out of tune.

Most travelers do not fly enough to have so severe a problem. But people who have crossed time zones rapidly often feel irritable and out of sorts for a few days after they arrive. Businessmen traveling to another continent, scientists flying to an international conference, and others who must fly long distances across time zones are often advised to schedule their arrival a day or two early, to give their bodies time to adjust before they try to do any important work.

The problems of upset biological clocks are especially serious for jet pilots and stewardesses. In one study conducted by the Federal Aviation Agency, several test groups were flown about the same number of miles in different directions. One group was flown through ten time zones from Oklahoma City to Manila, another group traveled in the opposite direction to Rome, while a third group was flown south to Chile. The third group was the only one that did not cross any time zones on the way. Just after landing, the members of all the groups were given a series of tests to show how fast they could react. Each person had to punch a telegraph key as quickly as possible after a light flashed on. Both groups that had been flown across time zones had much longer reaction times in comparison to the results of tests given before the flight. But the group that was flown about the same distance south, without crossing any time zones, reacted just as quickly to the light flashes as they had before the flight.

Airline officials are understandably concerned about the effects that upsets of biological clocks may have on airline pilots, for the lives of all the passengers and crew depend upon their skills. This is the primary reason why there are strict rules about how long a crew member may remain on duty without rest, and how much time there must be between flight assignments. But such upsets can also occur in many phases of our daily life.

The study of the many rhythms of the body is already suggesting ways that we can work and live more happily and efficiently. It has been found in studies on animals that drugs and other influences have different effects, depending on the time of day they are administered. If a rat is given the narcotic drug sodium pentobarbital during the day, for example, it will rapidly fall unconscious and remain so for a long time. The same dose of the drug given at night, when the rat is normally active, will have much less of an effect. X-rays, on the other hand, may kill mice at night at doses that would only make them sick during the daytime. In experiments at the skin allergy clinic of the Rothschild Foundation in Paris, French physicians found that antihistamines had quite different effects on human volunteers, depending on the time of day that they were injected.

Now physicians, led by Franz Halberg of the University of Minnesota Medical School, are beginning to realize that they must also learn to consider the inner clocks of their patients when they prescribe treatments. In this way, they could give drugs at the time when they are most effective and schedule operations for the time when the patient's own body defenses are strongest.

Studies of biological clocks can also point the way to more effective ways of working. U. S. Navy and Air Force researchers are testing groups of volunteers who live and work in sealed chambers for a month at a time, setting their own schedules or working on new work and sleep patterns, such as four hours on duty alternating with four hours at rest. Biotelemetry devices, such as those used to monitor the health of astronauts in space, keep the researchers informed about how the body systems of the volunteers are adapting to their schedules. All these studies have helped to emphasize that regular periods of sleep are an inseparable part of the daily rhythms of life.

THREE
Sleep in the Animal World

Have you ever watched a pet dog sleeping? Sometimes, he lies stretched out quietly, seeming completely relaxed. At other times, he seems almost surely to be dreaming. He trembles fitfully. His nose twitches, and his ears suddenly perk up. He may moan and whimper and growl softly. His breathing is irregular—sometimes fast and shallow, and sometimes he barely seems to be breathing at all. You can see his eyes moving beneath his closed eyelids. His paws may twitch, as though he were trying to run. Then these movements cease, and he lies quietly again, snoring gently.

Anyone who has ever had a pet dog or cat or mouse knows that these animals do indeed sleep. But what about the rest of the animal kingdom? Do birds sleep? Reptiles? Insects? Or do only man and his closest relatives have the need to refresh themselves with sleep each day?

Practically every living creature pauses in its activities at least once in each twenty-four hours and seems to rest. At night, some fish lie quietly at the bottom, hidden among the rocks and sand, while others float unmoving at the surface. Butterflies hang head down on a blade of grass, their wings folded tightly until morning. A robin dozes the night away perched firmly on a branch, while an owl is out hunting at night and sleeps fitfully by day. The ringed snake comes out of its burrow to hunt at noon and is back again only two hours later, to rest for a solid twenty-two. A rabbit dozes lightly in its nest in the grass, taking as many as twenty short naps in a single twenty-four-hour span.

All these animals must rest. But do they really sleep, as we know it? At first glance, the answer to this question seems obvious. If an animal periodically stops its activities and remains quiet and unmoving—if it looks as though it is sleeping—then why not simply assume that it is indeed sleeping? The naturalist Julian Huxley, for example, describes the behavior of sleeping

The domestic cat is one animal that seems to enjoy long, quiet sleeps, especially in the daytime.

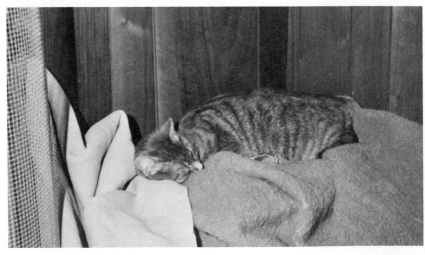

ALVIN AND VIRGINIA SILVERSTEIN

ants as strikingly similar to human practices. The ant lies down in a small hollow in the soil, with its legs drawn close to its body. After a few hours, it wakes, stretches and shakes all six legs, and strains its jaws wide just as though it were yawning.

The reluctance of many scientists to say that a particular animal does sleep and dream may seem overcautious. Yet it is understandable in the light of the recent history of the study of animal behavior. Until this century, naturalists tended to interpret their observations of animals' actions in terms of human thoughts and emotions. They saw and wrote about animals' actions as slyness and bravery, love and hate, selfishness and self-sacrifice. Then chemical and physical factors that determined many actions of animals were discovered. A mother bird's brooding and protecting her young could be explained by hormones and conditioned reactions, rather than an emotional feeling for her eggs and chicks. Like many revolutionary ideas, these new theories of animal behavior at first swung too far in the opposite direction. Instead of assuming human-like thoughts and emotions as the causes for animals' actions, many scientists now believed that animals could not be considered capable of any thought or emotion at all.

It was soon recognized that the new theories were too extreme. Our animal relatives share so many characteristics with us, down to the very chemicals of their bodies, that it is reasonable to assume that at least some of them can think and learn in much the same ways we do, can feel fear and affection, can sleep and dream.

But that still leaves the question, how can an observer be sure that an animal is sleeping? He can watch the animal and note whether it is active or lying quietly, and whether its eyes are open or closed. These factors are important clues, but they often are not enough. Horses and cows, for example, rarely close their eyes, and fishes and snakes cannot close them. Yet this does not necessarily mean that they do not sleep. Have you ever seen a cat dozing with one eye partly open? Even humans have occasionally been observed to sleep with one or both eyes partially open. Ani-

The wary rooster and some of his hens were startled awake by the photographer's approach, but others slept peacefully on.

mals do not necessarily lie down to sleep, either. Elephants, for example, often sleep standing up, with their tusks propped in the fork of a tree or in hollows of the wall of a zoo enclosure. (This is an understandable practice, considering the trouble an awakened elephant must take to hoist the enormous bulk of its body from a lying position. It must rock back and forth to build up momentum, or perhaps push against an anthill or other convenient rise in the ground.)

Another useful criterion is the animal's responsiveness to its environment. The expression "dead to the world" is often an apt description of the human or animal sleeper. He ignores lights, sounds, and other stimuli that he would ordinarily respond to while awake. A. E. Verrill reports some intriguing observations of fish at night in an aquarium at Woods Hole, Massachusetts. Fish of various types ceased their normal activities each night and took unusual body positions. Sometimes there was a characteristic color change that helped to camouflage them in the night waters. The filefish, for example, lay motionless at an angle, leaning against a stone or the glass wall of the aquarium. Its daytime mottled-brown and dark-green color changed to a light gray, with black fins and tail. Both the nighttime posture and the color change make the resting filefish resemble a weed, growing among the rocks. The porgy, too, turned from a bright silver in the daytime to a dull bronze with black stripes at night. Verrill tried turning on the lights of the aquarium suddenly. Immediately the porgies became active and turned back to their daytime silver color. The slightest vibrations of the air and water could also "awaken" the fish.

Observations such as these have prompted many scientists to conclude that fish, as well as amphibians and possibly reptiles, do not really sleep, as we experience it. Yet observations of animal behavior alone cannot fully resolve the question, for even humans are frequently quite responsive to external stimuli during certain phases of their sleep. A human sleeper automatically adjusts his covers according to the temperature of the room, may not only hear but also reply intelligently to spoken questions without waking, and can wake instantly to a sound or smell that his mind interprets as danger.

The use of the electroencephalograph (EEG) to obtain recordings of the minute electrical impulses generated in the brain has brought a wealth of new information into the study of sleep, both in humans and in animals. EEG recordings have resolved many old questions and raised some intriguing new ones.

When a human volunteer enters a sleep laboratory, electrodes are glued or taped to his forehead and various parts of his body. With experimental animals, researchers can go a step farther. Tiny wires can be inserted into specific parts of the brain and various body muscles while the animal is under anesthesia. These wires are then connected by cables to an electroencephalograph, so that the brain signals, breathing, heartbeat, and muscle activity can all be recorded automatically. After the animals recover from the operation, they appear to be perfectly normal and do not seem to notice the implanted electrodes or the cables connecting them to the machine.

The sleep of several dozen animal species has now been studied in the laboratory, and some interesting patterns are beginning to emerge.

For example, sleep researchers have found that some animals are good sleepers in the laboratory, and others are poor sleepers. Man is one of the good sleepers. After one "get-acquainted" night, most people are able to sleep quite normally in a sleep laboratory, in spite of the unusual surroundings, the watching researchers, and the maze of trailing electrodes and wires attached to their

The opossum is one animal that sleeps well in the laboratory, despite the electrode fastened to its head.

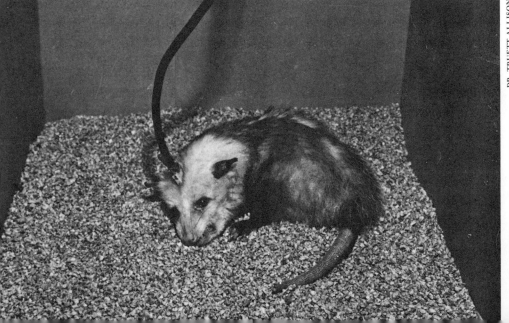

DR. TRUETT ALLISON

bodies. Sleep researchers Truett Allison and Henry Van Twyver report that man's close relatives, chimpanzees and macaque monkeys, are also good sleepers. After only a short adaptation in the laboratory, macaques sleep eight hours a day and chimpanzees sleep eleven hours a day. Cats are also good sleepers, sleeping up to fourteen hours a day in the laboratory. Moles need almost no adaptation before they are sleeping a regular eight hours a day, and ground squirrels sleep deeply about fourteen hours out of every twenty-four.

Hoofed animals, on the other hand, are generally poor sleepers. Sheep, goats, and donkeys take a long time—up to several months —before they will sleep in the laboratory at all. (Unlike man, these hoofed mammals are able to get along without sleep for long periods without any apparent harm.) Even when they are well adapted, these animals do not get much sleep. The donkey, for example, sleeps only about four hours a day. Rabbits and guinea pigs, too, are nervous and excitable animals that may take up to a few months to adapt to sleeping in the laboratory. Surprisingly, a member of the monkey family, the baboon, was also found to be a poor sleeper.

Is there any explanation for these wide differences in sleeping habits? How do the good sleepers differ from the poor sleepers, and what do they have in common with other members of the group? A comparison of the ways of life of each of the animals reveals a logical explanation for their sleeping habits. Nearly all of the good sleepers are predators, which have resting places secure from their enemies. The mole, for example, is a carnivore that lives in a network of underground burrows. The ancestors of the domestic cat were hunters, with few enemies to fear. The same holds for dogs, which are also good sleepers in the lab. Macaques are strong fighters. At night they take shelter in the leafy tops of tall trees, and they are light enough to climb easily to thin branches, where any night-prowling predators cannot follow them. The ground squirrel, too, has a safe place to sleep. Although it is a prey animal, when it is not out looking for seeds and other plant foods, the ground squirrel can retire to a snug burrow underground.

The poor sleepers are nearly all prey animals, which must be constantly on the alert for enemies even when they are resting. The wild ancestors of domestic sheep, goats, and donkeys lived and grazed in open grasslands. There was no shelter for them to hide in, and they were too big to make burrows underground. An ability to get along with little or no sleep was a valuable aid to their survival. Wild cavies (the ancestors of guinea pigs) and rabbits sometimes live in burrows, but frequently have nests in the grass on the surface. Even the baboon, a fierce fighter, must fear the leopard. This predator is a good climber and can easily follow the baboon into the trees in which it takes nighttime refuge.

Laboratory studies of sleeping animals thus agree with the logical premise that only animals with a safe sleeping place can afford the luxury of deep, long sleeps.

Just what EEG criteria help a researcher to determine whether or not an animal is actually sleeping? A typical recording of a cat's sleeping pattern provides a good illustration. Electrodes are placed around the eyes, to show eye movements; in the cerebral cortex, to record signals from the most highly developed portion of the brain; in the hippocampus, a region deep inside the brain that is involved with memory; and in the neck muscles, which support the animal's head.

While the cat is awake and alert, occasional large eye movements are recorded as it explores its surroundings. The tracing of electrical signals from the cerebral cortex shows many small, fast fluctuations. The tracing from the hippocampus looks like a rhythmic wave, as electrical pulses are recorded in synchronized bursts several times a second. The tracing of electrical activity from the neck muscles is a thick, ragged line, as the muscles work constantly to hold the cat's head up.

When the cat first falls asleep, there are marked changes in all these tracings. No more large eye movements are observed, although slow, rolling movements may be recorded. Large, slow waves, formed by many nerve cells working together, are recorded both from the cerebral cortex and from the hippocampus. From the appearance of these brain tracings, scientists have given this phase of sleep the name "slow-wave sleep." The tracings of electrical activity of the neck muscles show that there is still some muscle tone, but much less than when the cat was alert.

After a few minutes, there is a new change in the EEG tracings. The cat's eyes can be seen to move rapidly and jerkily under its closed eyelids, and these irregular and jerky movements are re-

EEG tracings of a cat during periods of wakefulness and of sleep

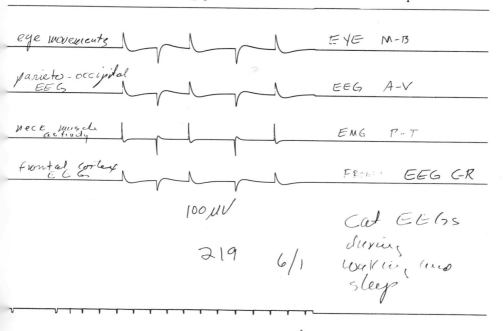

flected in the tracings. The tracings of brain activity now look quite similar to those recorded while the animal was awake. Yet the muscle tracing shows that muscle tone has disappeared completely. The cat's body is limp. This seems a paradox—an apparently alert mind in a clearly sleeping body. The cat has entered a new phase of sleep, which some sleep researchers refer to as paradoxical sleep.

After a time, the EEG tracings show that the cat's sleep has passed back into the slow-wave phase. The two types of sleep alternate until the animal awakens. With minor variations, the same pattern is observed in a wide variety of animals, including man. Both cats and humans, as well as the other good sleepers that have been studied, spend roughly a quarter of their sleeping time in the paradoxical phase. (Sleep researchers who concentrate on man more often use the term REM sleep, coined from the *R*apid *E*ye *M*ovements observed. But many animal researchers prefer the term "paradoxical sleep," since it is also observed in some animal species that do not show the rapid eye movements.) Hoofed mammals and other poor sleepers usually show a very small proportion of paradoxical sleep, perhaps 5 percent or so of their total sleeping time.

These findings support one of the major theories on the role that paradoxical sleep plays in the lives of animals. Frederic Snyder of the National Institute of Mental Health calls paradoxical sleep the "third state of existence." He suggests that periods of paradoxical sleep work as a sort of "sentinel" mechanism, bringing the animal out of the deep phase of slow-wave sleep so that it can inspect its environment for danger from time to time. An animal is much more easily aroused during paradoxical sleep than during slow-wave sleep, and it becomes fully alert and ready to react to potential dangers much more rapidly. Insecure sleepers tend to awaken during periods of paradoxical sleep, and these recurring periods of lighter sleep help to ensure that they will not sleep too long. Good sleepers tend to slip back into deep sleep

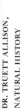

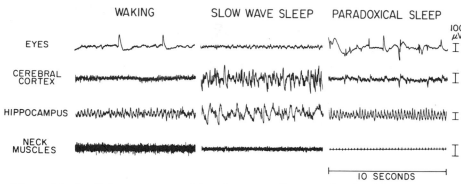

Three kinds of sleep, as traced by the EEGs of a man in the lab

after the paradoxical phase. But even humans and other good sleepers sleep fitfully, in short catnaps, in times of special danger.

The laboratory observations of good and poor sleepers also seem to support another theory of the meaning of paradoxical sleep. According to this theory, paradoxical sleep is a means of helping the unborn animal to develop its nervous system so that it will be able to cope with coordinated activities after birth. After birth, the eyes, ears, nose, and other sense organs constantly bombard the brain and spinal cord with a bewildering array of stimuli—sights, sounds, smells, tastes, touches. But the world inside the womb is a dull and unchanging one. There is no light, no temperature change; sounds are muffled, and sudden shocks and jars are muted to gentle vibrations. If the nerve circuits are to develop, they must get stimuli from somewhere; stimuli cannot come from outside, but are provided from within, by the brain. In the unborn animal, periods of paradoxical sleep can thus serve as times of exercise for the nervous system, helping to prepare it for the world after birth.

This theory of paradoxical sleep was developed on the basis of observations that newborn mammals, whether cat or rat or human, spend more time in paradoxical sleep than adults of the same species. Human infants, for example, spend about half of their sleeping time in paradoxical sleep; premature infants have an even higher proportion of paradoxical sleep.

If the theory is correct, we would expect animals born in a more highly developed state to have less paradoxical sleep than animals born in a very undeveloped, dependent form. This is exactly what is observed. Newborn kittens are hairless, their eyes sealed shut, unable to do anything for themselves except to suckle their mother's milk. Human babies are also extremely dependent for a long time after birth. The young of both these species spend a large amount of time in paradoxical sleep, with the proportion of this type of sleep gradually decreasing as more stimuli are available from outside. A newborn guinea pig, on the other hand, is fully formed and alert at birth, able to run about and feed within minutes after emerging from its mother's body. The young of hoofed mammals, too, are born in a well-developed state, able to stand and move about soon after birth. And it is precisely the young of these species that have far smaller amounts of paradoxical sleep.

These two theories of paradoxical sleep do not exclude each other—it is not a matter of choosing which is correct. It is quite likely that a mechanism serving a useful function in the animal's early development could persist and serve an equally valuable use in later life. There is much evidence to indicate that paradoxical sleep has another important offshoot; for this is the phase of sleep associated with dreaming.

There is no longer any doubt that the paradoxical, or REM, stage of sleep is the phase associated with dreaming in humans. Sleep researchers have established this by a very simple method: they wake sleepers in different phases of their sleep and ask them if they remember dreaming. Sleepers awakened in the REM stage nearly always recite a dream, while sleepers awakened from slow-wave sleep generally do not recall dreaming.

But how do you establish whether an animal is dreaming? A

This colt was able to stand and move around almost immediately after birth. Such animals need smaller amounts of paradoxical sleep than the young of species that are dependent on the mother for relatively long periods after birth.

sleep researcher cannot awaken a cat and ask what it is thinking about. It may look as though it is having a dream, but how can a human observer determine what is actually going on in the cat's mind?

For a time, it seemed that determining whether animals really dream or not was an insuperable problem. But recently some convincing evidence has been accumulated to indicate that in this phase of life, too, we are not alone.

In one experiment, for example, monkeys were trained to press a lever whenever pictures were flashed on a screen. If they failed to press the lever when a picture was showing, they received an electric shock, and they quickly mastered the idea. Then the researchers discovered that the monkeys were also pressing the lever in their sleep. This happened only during the paradoxical phase of sleep, and it occurred even though the monkeys' eyes were tightly closed and there was no real picture on the screen. It seemed that the monkeys were reacting to pictures inside their minds—dreams.

Monkeys are so closely related to humans that it is not surprising to find evidence that they dream as we do. But what about animals less closely related to us? Experiments on cats indicate that these animals, too, can dream.

During paradoxical sleep, an animal's muscle tone disappears, and its body is limp and relaxed. Scientists can locate the brain center that suppresses muscle tone and are able to disconnect it, leaving the rest of the brain intact. When this operation is performed on a cat, the results are striking. As soon as the animal enters the paradoxical phase of sleep, it behaves as though it were awake. It walks about, stalks imaginary prey, sits and follows an unseen object with its eyes—and all this time the EEG tracings show that it is deeply asleep.

Animal studies have cast new light on the nature and functions of paradoxical sleep, and they also are providing new insights into the nature of slow-wave sleep and its relationship to the paradoxical phase.

Truett Allison and Henry Van Twyver report on a series of experiments with intriguing implications on the evolution of sleep in the animal kingdom. It is believed that both the birds and the mammals developed separately from reptile ancestors, about two hundred million years ago. There is some evidence that reptiles do not truly sleep, although they do have periods of rest each day, in which they are quiet and unmoving. Yet all the birds and all the mammals studied in the laboratory have been shown actually to sleep, both by observations of behavior and by EEG tracings.

Birds vary greatly in their sleeping habits. Many birds sleep at night, firmly perched on a tree branch. At first glance, it might seem that the relaxation of muscle tone that occurs during sleep would cause a dozing bird to topple off its perch. It is saved from this fate by a fortunate adaptation of body structure. In a bird's leg, a strong tendon runs from the thigh muscle over the knee, down the shank, around the ankle, and under the bird's toes. When the bird settles down for the night, it bends its knees, and the tendons are pulled tight. Its toes are so firmly wrapped around the branch that the bird cannot be dislodged from its perch.

Even when a bird has built a nest, it usually does not use it for sleeping unless it is actively incubating eggs or raising young. Some birds, such as quail, roost on the ground, grouped together in a ring with all their tails together. Storks and herons sleep standing up, balanced on one leg. Ducks can sleep both on land and on the water. They sleep with their bills tucked into the feathers at the base of one wing, as many birds do. As a duck sleeps floating on the water, it may lazily paddle with one foot,

This sleeping bird has a firm grip on its perch.

ROGER KERKHAM

keeping its body in gentle motion. Ducks can sleep so soundly on the water that they have sometimes been found frozen into the ice on a pond after a sudden temperature drop during the night. Perhaps the most curious sleeping habits among birds are those of swifts, which can actually sleep in the air. E. Weitnauer, observing a colony of swifts with the aid of an airplane, discovered that in good weather these birds can spend the night riding rising columns of warm air.

The bird sleepers observed in the laboratory have shown clear signs of both slow-wave and paradoxical sleep. So have all the higher mammals studied, from chimpanzees to hedgehogs, bats to sheep, and mice to elephants and pilot whales. Allison and Van Twyver wondered at what stage of evolution these phases of sleep first appeared, and whether they developed together or separately.

It is obviously impossible to deduce from fossils whether a particular dinosaur or other extinct animal slept or not, much less the type and length of its sleeps. The fact that modern reptiles apparently do not experience true sleep suggests that this mechanism may have evolved after the bird and mammal offshoots branched off from the reptilian family tree. (This, in turn, indicates that the birds and mammals developed the ability to sleep independently, rather than inheriting it from a common ancestor.)

The first mammals are believed to have been reptile-like in some ways. The only survivors of this branch of the mammal group are two species, the duck-billed platypus and the echidna. Both are warm-blooded, hairy animals that feed their young with milk. But their young are hatched from leathery-shelled, reptilian-like eggs. Both are native to Australia, an island continent that was apparently cut off from the mainland before the higher mammals developed.

After the egg-laying mammals came the marsupials. These are the pouched mammals, whose young are born in an extremely undeveloped state and complete their development in a pouch in the mother's body. A number of marsupials, including kangaroos and wombats, have survived in Australia, but the only member of this group still living in the rest of the world is the opossum.

The most recent mammals to develop—perhaps a hundred million years or so ago—were the group to which humans belong, the placental mammals. The young of these mammals develop for long periods inside the mother's body, nourished by a connecting structure called the placenta.

Allison and Van Twyver hoped that by studying "modern fossils"—primitive egg-laying mammals and marsupials—they would find some clues to the evolution of sleep among the mammals. Opossums turned out to be quite typical mammal sleepers, showing patterns of both slow-wave and paradoxical sleep that were similar to those of placental mammals.

Echidnas, though, presented a different picture. The echidna normally spends much of its time digging underground, feeding on ants and other insects. In the laboratory, it proved to be a

The echidna, or spiny anteater, is a primitive mammal whose sleeping habits have helped scientists study the evolution of sleep among mammals.

good sleeper, adapting readily and sleeping up to twelve hours a day. But EEG tracings revealed that all this sleep was of the slow-wave type, alternating with quiet periods of nonsleep that were similar to the resting periods of reptiles. Not a single instance of paradoxical sleep was observed.

To rule out the possibility that the echidna's specialized way of life was the cause of its unique sleeping pattern, rather than its level of development, Allison and Van Twyver studied a placental mammal with a similar mode of living: the mole. The mole is even more adapted to life underground than the echidna, and it has extremely poor vision. But moles were found to have sleeping habits surprisingly like those of humans—they sleep about eight hours a day, and about a quarter of this is paradoxical sleep.

The sleep researchers thus conclude that the two phases of sleep apparently developed separately, with slow-wave sleep arising first among the primitive egg-laying mammals. Paradoxical sleep probably developed later, among the primitive marsupials.

This conclusion raises another intriguing question: why did two groups, the birds and the mammals, independently develop the habit of sleeping? Do they have anything else in common that might be linked with their sleeping patterns?

Birds and mammals share an important characteristic that is not possessed by any other group: an ability to maintain a constant body temperature even when the temperature of the environment varies. These animals are called warm-blooded, because their bodies stay warm even when it is cold outside. (Animals vary in their ability to withstand freezing temperatures.) Reptiles, amphibians, fishes, and all invertebrates (animals without backbones) are cold-blooded: their body temperatures stay approximately at the temperature of their environment. Cold-blooded animals are not always cold, by any means; fishes that swim in warm tropical waters, for example, have quite high body temperatures. But when external temperatures fall, the body temperature of a cold-blooded animal must follow.

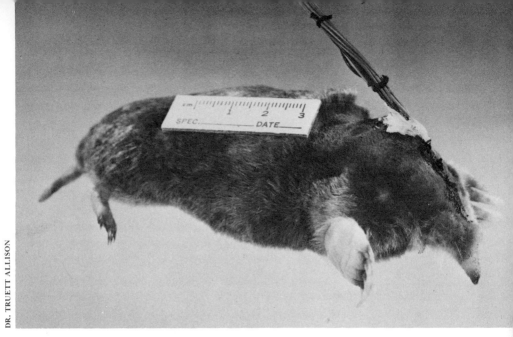

Lab experiments on this mole and others of his species indicate that the mole's sleeping habits are like those of humans.

Many of the chemical reactions of the body proceed most effectively at temperatures in the neighborhood of 37°C (which is 98.6°F, the human body temperature). Much higher than this, vital enzymes and other body chemicals are inactivated or destroyed, and the animal may die. At lower temperatures, vital reactions slow down, and the animal becomes sluggish and inactive. An animal that can keep its body temperature constant thus has an important built-in advantage in the struggle for life: it can remain active through all seasons of the year, can survive longer-term changes in climate, and can adapt to a variety of habitats.

The advantages of warm-bloodedness are balanced by an important disadvantage: keeping the body temperature constant is enormously expensive in terms of energy. The animal must continually replenish its energy supplies by feeding. A substantial saving of energy could be gained if there were some way of periodically turning down the body's "thermostat." Sleep provides just such a mechanism. Just how effective it can be is evident from a comparison of the shrew and the bat. Both are small, warm-blooded mammals. When they are active, both have an extremely high metabolic rate (the rate of the chemical reactions that go on in the body). The shrew is an excitable little animal that scurries about constantly in search of food. It can apparently get along with extremely little sleep. But it lives only two years. A bat of the same size sleeps up to twenty hours a day. During sleep, its body reactions slow down, and with this saving of energy it does not need to feed so voraciously. The difference in life spans is spectacular—the bat can live up to eighteen years. Thus it seems that sleep can actually prolong an animal's life.

Allison and Van Twyver believe that it is slow-wave sleep that serves the energy-saving function, for this is the only form observed in the warm-blooded echidna. Slow-wave sleep also makes up the bulk of birds' sleep and that of many other animals as well. This phase of sleep seems to be the most restful, as the paradoxical phase is accompanied by a speedup of activity in the nervous system and various other parts of the body.

FOUR
A Night's Sleep

Did you sleep well last night? Your answer to this question will be based on a number of things. An important factor will probably be how you felt when you awoke in the morning—cheerful and alert, or grouchy and irritable, perhaps still drowsy, with a feeling that you could have used a bit more sleep. Your reply will be colored, too, by memories of how long it took you to fall asleep. You may have had the impression of dropping off almost instantly, as soon as your head hit the pillow. Or perhaps it seemed forever, your mind busily turning over thoughts about the events of the day, worrying about an exam the next day, or weaving intricate details in the continuing story of your favorite daydream. You may have vague remembrances of awakening in the middle of the night, or of tossing and turning restlessly. Fragments of dreams may have lingered in your mind when you awoke, or perhaps came to you suddenly later, recalled by the events of the day. Or you may remember absolutely nothing from the time you first felt yourself drifting off until you opened your eyes in the morning.

Just what did happen during the eight hours or so that you "lost" last night? Did your thoughts simply turn off, like an electric light? Was your brain perhaps idling like an automobile engine, when the motor has been started but the transmission is still in neutral? Or did active thoughts somehow mysteriously continue, hidden from your awareness? What was your body doing during this time? Was it lying quietly or moving restlessly? What about your heartbeat, your breathing, the countless chemical reactions—did they go on in the same way as when you were awake, or were there changes in rate and intensity?

Is there any way to find out what really happens during the hidden life of sleep?

You cannot observe yourself sleeping. If you try, you will be doomed to frustration. Either your mind will remain so alert and vigilant that you will not fall asleep, or if sleep does overcome you, you will lose all awareness of your own condition, thus ending your observations before the state you wanted to observe has properly begun.

You can watch another person sleeping. You can note a series of changes as he closes his eyes and becomes progressively more relaxed. You may notice changes in his breathing; you may see him turn and shift his position, twitch from time to time, and perhaps mumble indistinct phrases. But what is happening inside the sleeper, what is going on in his mind and body, still remains largely a mystery.

Man has speculated on the nature of sleep for millennia. Any book of quotations has dozens or hundreds of entries relating to this mysterious part of life. But the scientific study of sleep did not really get started until the invention of an important tool: the electroencephalograph.

The name of the electroencephalograph is a combination of three roots. *Electro-* comes from "electricity." *Encephalo-* is taken from the Greek word "encephalon," meaning "the brain." *Graph* comes from another Greek word, meaning "to write." The elec-

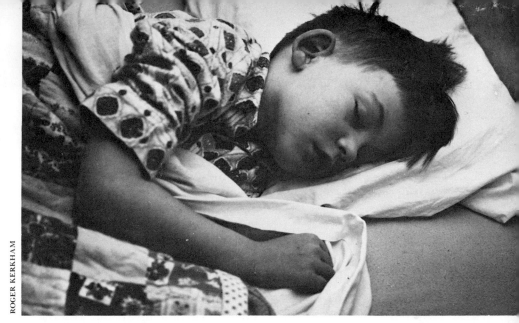

This boy seems quiet and peaceful in sleep, but one can't really tell what is going on inside his brain and his body.

troencephalograph, which scientists usually abbreviate as EEG, is thus a machine that measures electricity from the brain and writes down the results.

The brain is an awesome structure. Wrinkled and jelly-like, about the size of a grapefruit, a human brain has the ability to control and coordinate breathing and other vital processes of the body, to receive and analyze messages from the sense organs, to direct and monitor the actions of the muscles, and to think and plan, to remember and to learn from experience. This control center of the body contains billions of microscopic nerve cells, linked into an intricate network. Messages flash ceaselessly along the network of nerve cells of the brain, bringing new information, processing and correlating, and directing the body's activities. These messages are transmitted by means of electrochemical reactions, and, in the process, tiny potential differences or electrical charges are generated. These charges continually change and shift as the brain goes about its business. Together they combine to create patterns of electrical potential differences that can be detected even outside the skull, if sensitive-enough receivers are used.

This principle was discovered about a century ago by Richard Caton of Liverpool, England. He found that if he pasted two small silver discs, or electrodes, to the scalp of a rabbit, making an electrical connection by placing a bit of salty jelly between each electrode and the rabbit's skin, tiny changes in the electrical potential differences between the two points on the scalp could be observed. He demonstrated his discovery in 1875 at a meeting of the British Medical Association in Edinburgh, Scotland, using both rabbits and monkeys. But it was not until fifty years later that an Austrian psychiatrist, Hans Berger, established that the same kind of electrical potential differences can be observed over the human brain.

In the modern electroencephalograph, the tiny electrical signals from the electrodes are amplified and transmitted to a pen device that automatically traces out the voltage changes in zigzag recordings in ink on a roll of paper that moves continuously beneath it. Usually there is a row of pens, side by side, which register potential differences from different parts of the scalp, the movements of the eyes, and the electrical activity of various other muscles of the body as well. Other pens record the rate and depth of respiration and the heartbeat on the same roll of paper at the same time. An electroencephalogram is thus a long strip of paper (the roll may be a thousand feet long!) on which rows of squiggly lines trace out a record of the changes in the electrical activity of the subject's brain, along with his heart activity and breathing.

The electroencephalograph would thus seem to be an excellent tool for gaining some concrete information about what goes on inside a sleeper's body and brain. There is only one problem: could

As the volunteer subject sleeps, electrodes taped to his head, the researcher examines the patterns traced by the pens at the lower right, recording the impulses received by the EEG machine. Note that there are six sets of controls.

a normal person possibly fall asleep, much less sleep normally, in a strange laboratory room, with electrodes pasted to his face, head, and neck, a blood-pressure cuff clamped tightly around his arm or leg, trailing wires connecting him to a mysterious machine, and the unfamiliar sounds of researchers bustling about him?

Many volunteers for sleep experiments are convinced that they will not be able to fall asleep at all under these circumstances. Yet they generally find, to their surprise, that they do indeed drop off to sleep within a mere ten or fifteen minutes. (In fact, sleep researchers studying insomnia met an unexpected problem. After advertising for volunteers who habitually had trouble falling asleep at night, they discovered that their subjects often fell asleep in the laboratory far more rapidly than they did at home in their own beds!)

During the first night in the laboratory, a sleep-experiment volunteer may sleep fitfully. But after a night or two, he usually settles down; as he becomes accustomed to laboratory surroundings, his nightly EEG records display a pattern that is amazingly consistent and so characteristic of him that the watching researcher can often predict just what will happen next, as one phase of sleep blends into another.

There are many individual differences in EEG sleep patterns, variations according to age and sex, personality, mental and physical health, and simply from person to person. But some general patterns have emerged from the records of thousands of sleepers, and these patterns are so universal that sleep researchers are convinced that the nights of sleep that they watch in the laboratory really are normal nights' sleep.

At the three dozen or so sleep laboratories throughout the world, the night's "work" generally does not start for the subjects until about 10 P.M. But the research team has already been busy for hours, checking equipment to make sure all the electrical connections are tight, filling inkwells, and running various last-minute tests and preparations.

Now the subject arrives. He may be a college or medical student at the local university. He may have answered an ad in the newspaper, requesting volunteers with particular sleep problems or physical conditions. The majority of sleep studies have been conducted with young men of normal intelligence and health, but studies have also been made of sleep patterns in other groups—

women, infants and the aged, hospital patients with heart disease, ulcers, or psychiatric problems.

The subject's preparations for sleep are in some ways similar to his normal nightly habits. He washes and changes into pajamas and robe. But he is not yet ready to lie down in the bed conveniently prepared for him. First the electrodes must be attached. Carefully the experimenter marks out the proper places on the subject's face and head, swabs each one with pungent-smelling acetone, dabs on a bit of gel, and firmly tapes down the small metal electrodes. The array of color-coded wires trailing from the electrodes is then drawn through a ring at the top of the head. The subject may feel some alarm at all these preparations if this is his first time at the sleep lab, but the experimenter soothes him

Preparing the subject for a good night's sleep at a Brooklyn, New York, sleep lab

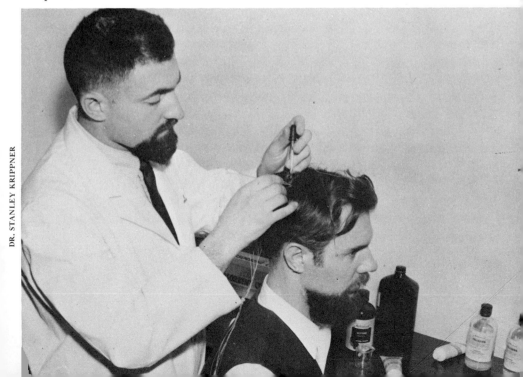

with a steady patter of commonplace conversation. By the time the last electrode is in place, the subject very likely is already drowsy.

The bed in the laboratory room is an ordinary one, with a pillow and bedclothes. Although the wire-leads from the electrodes are plugged into a board at the head of the bed, connected by cables to the EEG machine in the control room, they are long enough to permit the sleeper to move freely in bed. Close by is an intercom system and a tape-recorder microphone. A closed-circuit television camera may be mounted in a corner of the sound-proof room, or a mirror on one wall may actually be a one-way observation window, through which the experimenters can observe the sleeper's progress.

The subject settles his head on the pillow, and in the control room the EEG machine begins to whisper softly as it traces out the brain-wave rhythms. A moving drum rolls a seemingly endless strip of paper beneath the jittering pens. By the time the night is over, nearly half a mile of records will have been added to the fund of data on sleep.

The waking EEG is a jumble of rapid, irregular waves. Aimless thoughts drift through the subject's mind as he slowly relaxes. Falling asleep is not a sudden, "out-like-a-light" change, but rather a gradual transition through stages of decreasing awareness.

The subject has closed his eyes now, and the EEG is showing a new pattern, a regular rhythm of waves cresting about nine to twelve times a second. This is called the alpha rhythm, and it seems to characterize a state of pleasant, relaxed awareness. Zen Buddhists have been found to show an alpha rhythm while they are meditating, and, with the aid of EEG machines, people can be taught to recognize their own alpha rhythms by flashing a light or sounding a tone whenever its pattern appears. With some practice, they can hold this brain-wave pattern and even produce it at will.

But in the normal drifting into sleep, the alpha rhythm is a

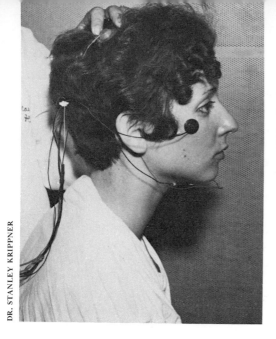

Here is a closeup view of the attachments that were made to one sleep subject. A blood-pressure cuff may be attached to her arm, too.

fragile state. A sudden noise, an errant thought that focuses the subject's attention, and the alpha rhythm dissolves, to be replaced again by the tight, irregular tracings of the wakeful mind.

The subject relaxes further, and the alpha waves grow smaller. Now he is in a drowsy state. His eyes are closed, and his body rests quietly. His body temperature is falling now. Vague thoughts and images are drifting through his mind. He is on the verge of sleep.

It would be very easy to arouse him now, and indeed, his own body may momentarily startle him into awareness at this point. Have you ever noticed a sudden, convulsive jerk of your whole body just as you were on the point of falling asleep? You may have had a sensation of falling along with it, and a sudden surge of anxiety. This "startle" reaction is called a myoclonic jerk, and it is the result of a tiny burst of activity in the brain that resembles an epileptic seizure. But it is nothing to fear, for it is a common occurrence at the threshold of normal sleep.

The subject may not notice the brief interruption of the my-oclonic jerk, or he may lapse quickly back to drowsiness after his momentary arousal. Now he is drifting over the borderline. His EEG shows that the alpha rhythm has dwindled away, except for occasional bursts. The pens scribble out a fast, irregular pattern, constantly changing. The subject may have a feeling of floating or drifting along with idle thoughts. He would still be easy to awaken, and once awake he would probably insist that he had not been asleep at all, only "thinking." But striking changes are occurring in his body. His muscles are relaxing, and his heart is beating more slowly. His breathing is more even. He does not realize it, but he is now blind! If his eyes were open and a brightly

An EEG of the wakeful state. Calibrations at bottom are one-second intervals.

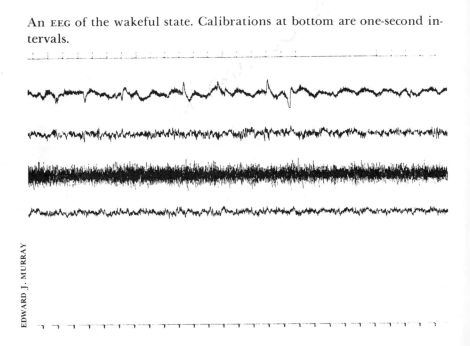

EDWARD J. MURRAY

lighted object were held in front of him, he would not see it at all. Two sleep researchers at the University of Chicago, Allen Rechtschaffen and David Foulkes, have demonstrated this effect by studying the sleep of people whose eyes were firmly taped open. You might think that a person would have difficulty falling asleep under such conditions, but the subjects were able to adjust with little difficulty. Time after time, a member of the team would hold a lighted object, such as a sign or a coffeepot, in front of the subject's open eyes during this light, first phase of sleep. After a few seconds, the sleeper would be awakened by a call over the loudspeaker. The subject would generally relate some fragment of dreamy imaginings, stoutly insisting that he had not yet fallen asleep—yet he would be completely unaware that a lighted object had been held up right in front of his eyes.

Sleep researchers call this light, first phase of sleep stage 1. This stage usually does not last very long, only a few minutes. If the sleeper is not disturbed, stage 1 sleep quickly flows into a new, deeper sleep: stage 2.

Now the EEG pens in the control room begin to chatter a bit. The brain waves trace out quick bursts of zigzags spaced very close together, which grow rapidly larger and then smaller again as the voltage rises and falls. The ink record of these bursts resembles a wire spindle, and sleep researchers refer to them as sleep spindles. The pens tracing the subject's eye movements, which traced out nearly solid lines during stage 1, now show that the eyes are rolling slowly. They are not focused; if his eyes were open, he would not see anything. Vague thoughts and dreams, though not clear images, are drifting through the subject's mind. He has been solidly asleep for more than ten minutes now, but he is still fairly easy to awaken. And he is still likely to insist, if roused, that he has not yet been asleep.

If the sleeper is undisturbed, he will drift gradually into stage 3, a deeper phase of sleep. Large, slow waves are scattered among the spindles and small, irregular brain-wave tracings. These slow waves are called delta waves; they come about one per second, and their voltage may be five times as great as the alpha rhythm. The sleeper's muscles are very relaxed now. His heart rate has slowed down further, and his blood pressure is falling. His breathing is steady and even. He is difficult to awaken now—to bring him out of stage 3 will take a rather loud noise or an insistent repetition of his name.

Gradually the subject's sleep blends into a still deeper form, stage 4. The sleep spindles disappear, and the brain waves show only the large, slow delta waves. The subject lies still, and his muscles are very relaxed. He is breathing slowly and evenly, and his heart rate and temperature are low. It is very difficult to awaken him now. Even if he is shaken, or if his name is called loudly, it will take him several seconds to rouse. When he does finally awaken, he will probably say that nothing was passing through his mind. He may have been mumbling softly only a moment or two before, but he will not remember it.

If the subject is prone to sleepwalking or bed-wetting, an episode may occur during the phase of stage 4 sleep. Yet if he is awakened, he will have no memory of the episode at all.

Now it is about an hour and a half since the subject went to sleep. He is soundly in the depths of stage 4, and he has spent a large fraction of his sleeping time so far in this deep stage of sleep. But then there is a change. Sleep spindles begin to punctuate the brain-wave tracings. The slow delta waves fade away. The subject is drifting upward, into lighter stages of sleep. He seems to be awakening.

Suddenly there is a crashing clatter of the EEG pens. The subject stirs and rolls over in bed. As the EEG tracings calm down, the brain-wave records show a pattern of rapidly changing zigzags, small and irregular. The tracings resemble the patterns of wakefulness, and early sleep researchers thought that they represented actual periods of waking. But they were mistaken. The subject is

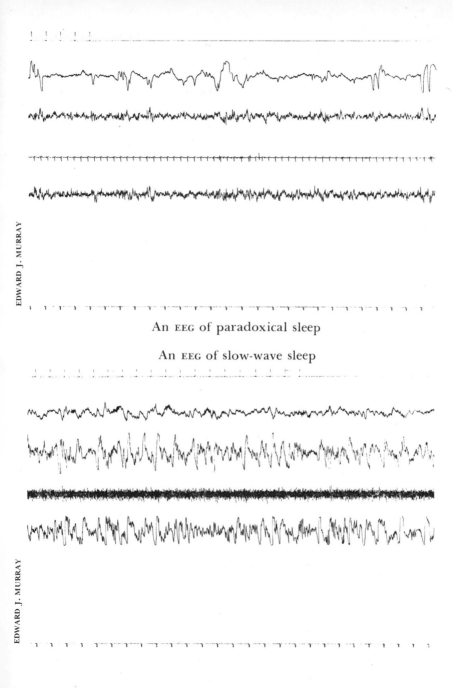

An EEG of paradoxical sleep

An EEG of slow-wave sleep

EDWARD J. MURRAY

EDWARD J. MURRAY

still deeply asleep. And now something new is added to the EEG record for the night.

With rapid darts, the pens signaling eye movement slash out a pattern of peaks. The eyes are moving back and forth, and they are moving together, as though the subject were watching a movie. His eyes can be seen to be moving quite clearly beneath his closed eyelids. Now the other EEG pens begin to trace out a unique story. Breathing is rapid, shallow, uneven. The heart rate and blood pressure fluctuate widely. Stimulating hormones from the adrenal glands flood the sleeper's body. The temperature within his brain rises.

The EEG records show a storm of activity taking place within the sleeper. Yet his body is completely limp. His head and neck muscles are so relaxed that they would not support his head. If he is awakened suddenly, he may think that he is paralyzed.

The sleeper is in the midst of a peculiar phase of sleep that researchers generally refer to as REM sleep, because of the *R*apid *E*ye *M*ovements that characterize it. He is not easy to rouse, but a loud buzzer or bell will do it. If he is awakened, he is very likely to relate a vivid and detailed dream.

The wide fluctuations of the subject's heart rate, blood pressure, and breathing during REM periods would seem to suggest that he is having a violent nightmare and is in a state of extreme fright. Yet the dream he relates when he is awakened may be quite pleasant and peaceful.

Left undisturbed, the sleeper spends about ten minutes in this first REM period of the night. Then the rapid eye movements stop, and he begins to drift downward again, passing successively through the stages of sleep to the deepest, stage 4, once more. After a time—about an hour and a half after the first REM episode —the cycle repeats itself again, and there is a new REM period. This one is longer, and if the subject is awakened, the dream he relates will be more vivid and detailed.

On through the night it goes like a roller coaster, up to the

REM stage and down again to the deeper stages of sleep. At each turn of the cycle, the REM episodes become longer, and the phases of sleep between them less deep. Depending on the individual and the length of time he sleeps, there will be from four to six REM periods during the night, roughly an hour and a half apart. Most of the stage 4 sleep is packed into the first half of the night; indeed, the last cycle or two will probably have no stage 4 sleep at all.

Have you ever heard the saying that the best sleep comes before midnight? Fortunately, the dire implications of that proverb for people who normally go to bed at twelve o'clock or later are unfounded. But in times past, when people commonly went to bed shortly after sundown, there was more than a little truth to the proverb. If you went to bed at eight, you would indeed get in most of your stage 4 sleep before midnight, and sleep researchers believe that this deepest phase of sleep does most to restore and refresh the body.

In the sleep lab, the night wears on. The sleeper periodically stirs and turns in his bed. The rolls of paper in the EEG machine have been changed, and the monotonous scribbling goes on. In the wee hours of the morning, somewhere between 3 and 5 A.M., the sleeper's body temperature hits its lowest point and begins to rise again. The dreams he relates when he is awakened during REM periods are rich and detailed, filled with color and bizarre happenings. The sleep researchers are beginning to show signs of fatigue. They may be approaching their own temperature lows, and their bodies crave sleep. Watching the sleeper in the bedroom, they sip coffee and fight to stay alert.

At last, the long night is over. The experimenters wearily strip off the electrodes as they ask the volunteer, "How did you sleep?" He dresses and leaves, and the researchers are faced with the prospect of snatching a few hours of sleep for themselves before returning to the demands of daily living—their teaching jobs, setting up the equipment for the next run, and the monu-

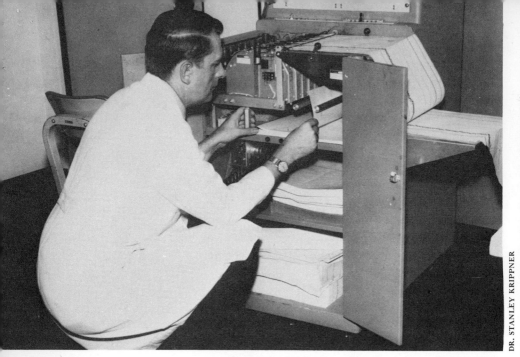

Checking the machine at the end of a long night

mental task of analyzing the two thousand feet or so of EEG records that the night's session has yielded.

The discovery that EEG tracings provided an objective record against which other observations of sleepers could be compared was an enormous spur to sleep research. Now there is a means of probing into such areas of study as why we sleep, the nature of dreams, the causes of bed-wetting and sleepwalking, and the usefulness of drugs to produce sleep. Researchers observe the effects of depriving people of sleep, or of certain phases of sleep. They probe into the workings of the brain and its biochemistry. Each new discovery raises new questions, and gradually many of the mysteries of sleep are being unraveled.

FIVE
The Land of Dreams

What did you dream last night? Can you remember? Some people can recall portions of their nighttime fantasy life in vivid detail. Others claim that they never dream at all. Yet studies in sleep laboratories have revealed that people normally dream as many as four or five or even six separate times each night.

What are your dreams like? Bits and pieces of your waking experiences are woven into them: people you know or used to know, houses, cars, clothes; trips you have taken; everyday situations in the classroom, the sports field, or at work; things you have read about, strange animals, foreign places. Most of these are things you might idly think about in the moments before you go to sleep, or in a spell of daytime woolgathering. But there are differences between a dream and a train of idle thoughts. In a dream, the usual logic that your brain follows often does not seem to apply; the laws that normally govern events in the world are suspended. In a dream, you may at one moment be sitting comfortably in your living room, and then, without any real transition, you are somewhere else—scuba diving in the Caribbean, trekking across the snow-swept Russian steppes, or riding downtown on the bus. Things change suddenly and mysteriously—a purring tabby cat may suddenly be a fire-breathing dragon or a whistling locomotive. Your own vantage point may shift abruptly —you may seem to be nothing more than an interested observer, then you suddenly realize that you are one of the main characters in the drama, either in your own likeness or in the guise of someone of a different appearance, age, or even sex. There is often an emotional content in dreams—a feeling of intense pleasure, or worry, or chilling fear.

Have you ever dreamed that something—a tiger, perhaps, or a fanciful mythical beast, or some vaguely defined horror—was pursuing you? On you fled through the mysterious dreamland, until there was no longer anywhere to run and the beast was almost upon you. You tried to scream, but no sound came out. In a second it would be upon you, but you were paralyzed. . . . And then you awoke, shaken and drenched in sweat, unable to move for a moment, unsure exactly where you were. In a few moments your muscles regained their tone, and you stirred restlessly, poised for a time in wakefulness, a little afraid to go back to sleep lest the vivid dream monster might still be lurking in wait.

Dreams have been reported since the beginnings of recorded history, and indeed, studies of animals suggest that the first apelike ancestors of man undoubtedly dreamed, too. Yet it is perhaps a peculiarly human trait to search ceaselessly for the meaning of dreams. It seemed logical that all this frenzied mental activity must have *some* meaning.

In ancient times, it was generally believed that dreams were a portent of future events. These were not foretold directly, but were disguised in symbols. Four-thousand-year-old papyrus records from Egypt instruct the reader on the interpretation of certain dream symbols. A dream of distant crowds, for example, was a warning of death to come.

The disguised nature of dream messages required great skill from the would-be interpreter. The oracles of the ancient Greeks were specialists in interpreting dreams. One of the most famous of the ancient dream interpreters was Joseph, whose story is related in the Bible.

Joseph was a vivid dreamer, and his talents showed themselves early. He was his father's favorite child, and his elder brothers were already jealous of him when he dreamed a special dream:

". . . For, behold, we were binding sheaves in the field, and lo, my sheaf arose, and also stood upright; and, behold, your sheaves stood round about, and made obeisance to my sheaf."

The symbolism in this dream was obvious even to his brothers.

"And his brethren said to him, 'Shalt thou indeed reign over us? Or shalt thou indeed have dominion over us?' And they hated him yet the more for his dreams. . . .'"

The jealousy of Joseph's brothers caused them to sell him into slavery. A series of misadventures landed him in prison in Egypt, from which he won release by his talents in interpreting dreams. He came to the attention of the Pharaoh, who was then troubled by a puzzling dream:

"Behold, Pharaoh stood by the river. And behold there came up out of the river seven well-favored kine and fat-fleshed; and they fed in a meadow. And behold, seven other kine came up after them out of the river, ill-favored and lean-fleshed; and stood by the other kine on the brink of the river. And the ill-favored and lean-fleshed kine did eat up the seven well-favored and fat kine."

In another version of the dream, the fat and lean cattle were replaced by seven fat and seven lean ears of corn. None of the Egyptian dream experts could agree on a satisfactory interpretation of the dreams. Joseph's explanation was that the country was due for seven years of good harvests, followed by seven years of drought and famine. He suggested that Pharaoh prepare for the seven lean years by stockpiling grain from the abundant harvests of the seven good years.

Joseph explains the dream to Pharaoh, in a drawing by Raphael.

Such was Pharaoh's faith in the power of dreams that he gave Joseph sweeping executive powers to carry out his proposed "seven-year plan." Events proved Joseph's interpretation to be correct, and in the famine that followed the seven good years, Egypt was the only country in the region where food could be obtained. Joseph's brothers were forced to journey into Egypt seeking to buy food, and, not realizing who he was, they did indeed bow down to him.

Many modern people would scoff at the idea that dreams could foretell the future. Yet in nearly any newstand you can find paperback "dream books" on sale, providing lists of symbols purporting to tell a person how to guide his life on the basis of what he dreamed last night.

But for the most part, the predictive role of dreams has been relegated to a not-very-respectable status in scientific and intellectual circles. Since the beginning of this century, modern thought on the matter of dream interpretation has been dominated by a quite different theory, that of Sigmund Freud.

Freud was a physician in Austria around the turn of the century. He had been trained as a neurophysiologist, well versed in what was then known of the workings of the nervous system. From his own experiences and from work with his patients, he came to the conclusion that many ailments, both mental and physical, have their roots in upsetting experiences and conflicts

Sigmund Freud, in an etching by Ferdinand Schlutzer

PRINCETON UNIVERSITY

that occurred in early childhood. As the years pass, these early conflicts may become hidden away inside the mind, so that the patient himself sincerely does not remember them. Freud developed techniques for delving into a patient's problems and gradually revealing their deep-seated causes; once these causes are out in the open, the patient can be taught to accept and cope with them. Freud's techniques were the basis for the modern practice of psychoanalysis.

Early in his studies and observations, Sigmund Freud became fascinated by the subject of dreams. He regarded these fragments of mental fantasy as unique keys to the hidden life of the mind, keys that could be used to unlock the conflicts buried at the root of his patients' problems. He saw dreams as a "royal road to the unconscious." Collecting dreams and analyzing them systematically, Freud gradually built up a theory of the meaning of dreams, which he published in 1900 in a book, *The Interpretation of Dreams.*

In Freud's view, dreams have two main functions: an attempt to fulfill unconscious wishes that the person might be completely unaware of in his normal waking state, and the protection of sleep, guarding the person from being aroused in the middle of the night. These two functions might sometimes be at cross-purposes. Suppressed wishes, which the person dares not express while awake, are often violently aggressive or sexual; if these were too obviously expressed even during sleep, they might create anxiety in the sleeper and so awaken him. As a result, these unconscious wishes often express themselves in a disguised form, couched in symbols. An apple, for example, might symbolize a mother's breast, and a dream of bathing would be a reenactment of the experience of birth. Unconscious wishes may be distorted in other ways to protect the sleeper from anxiety. Several different thoughts may be blended or condensed into a single image. A disturbing emotion might be displaced to some other object. A girl frightened of her father, for example, might dream of a robber coming after her with a blackjack, or a tiger chasing her in the jungle. The guilt she might feel at having fearful feelings toward her father, whom she feels she should love and trust, is soothed by giving her fearful feelings a more acceptable object.

As a result of these distortions, in Freud's view, a dream has two levels of meaning. The manifest content of the dream is the actual form the dream experience takes, expressed in symbols. These symbols hide the latent content of the dream, its hidden, underlying meaning. The psychoanalyst tries to find the significance of the dream symbols and go beyond them to dig out the dream's latent content. In doing so, he must find ways to weed out elaborations the patient may introduce in relating his dreams. The patient may consciously change parts of dream memories in the retelling, in order to hide some aspect that he is afraid to reveal, or he may unconsciously distort or embroider the tale, filling in bits that he does not remember clearly, juggling events to make them conform better to the waking mind's concepts of logic and coherence.

An important technique that the psychoanalyst uses in the analysis of dreams is free association. After noting down the patient's narrative, he divides the dream into its elements and then questions the patient about each one individually, asking him to say the first thing that comes into his mind as each dream element is mentioned. These links to the workings of the patient's mind help the psychoanalyst to determine better what each specific symbol means to him.

Another noted psychoanalyst, Carl Jung, worked with Freud for several years. Jung, too, was fascinated by the subject of dreams and the meaning that they might hold. He formulated his own theories of dream interpretation, and his differences with Freud on this subject were one of the causes of a split between the two men. Jung believed that dreams are basically symbolic, and their main function is to compensate for aspects of the dreamer's personality that have been neglected in his conscious life.

He believed that the origin of the dream symbols lay not in the patient's own early life, but rather in inborn thought patterns common to all mankind. He pointed to recurring themes and symbols found in the religion and folklore of peoples all over the world. Jung held that dreams express themselves in the form of symbols not because the dreamer must disguise his true desires, but because dreams reflect fragments of memories shared by all members of the human race, memories that can express themselves only in the form of symbols. He saw dreams as an attempt to reveal, rather than to conceal, what is in the unconscious mind. His followers use mythology, comparative religion, and history in their attempts to interpret dreams.

When a person awakens in the morning and jots down memories of last night's dreams to repeat at his next appointment with his psychoanalyst, does he really have a representative record of his mental activity while asleep? Is there any way to find out what is really happening inside the mind of the dreamer, while it is happening? Early sleep researchers tried setting an alarm clock to wake themselves up at various times during the night, with a pad of paper by the bedside to record any dreams they might recall. But this is a rather tiring and not very effective method.

The first new, truly scientific approach to the problem came in the early 1950s, with a breakthrough discovery at the University of Chicago. By 1952, the EEG machine had been used for some time to study the brain reactions of a variety of people both in the waking and in the sleeping state. Pioneer sleep physiologist Nathaniel Kleitman was conducting round-the-clock studies of the sleeping habits of a group of infants, with the aid of a graduate student, Eugene Aserinsky. One afternoon, Aserinsky noticed that the eyeballs of the sleeping babies seemed to be moving rapidly under their closed eyelids. Both eyes moved together, just as though the infants were looking at something. After a time, these rapid eye movements subsided, but then, after about an hour, they began again. As the babies slept, periods of rapid eye movements were repeated again and again, in cycles of about an hour.

Intrigued, Kleitman and Aserinsky decided to see whether rapid eye movements were also observed in adults. They were joined in the new experiments by a medical student, William Dement. Adding a set of electrodes on the eyelids to the standard assortment, the research team discovered that these rapid eye movements were indeed observed in all sleepers. In adults, the REM episodes recurred just as regularly as they did in children, but the cycles were approximately an hour and a half in duration. The rapid eye movements were always accompanied by a quite distinct, rapid pattern of brain waves, which showed a startling resemblance to the EEG tracings of waking. This was a great contrast to the slow waves of deep sleep that preceded the REM periods.

The rapid back-and-forth eye movements looked very much like the movements a person's eyes make when he is awake and reading a newspaper column or watching the action on a movie screen. In addition, the sleeper shows clear signs of apparent great excitement during REM episodes—irregular heartbeat, shallow and uneven breathing, twitchings of the hands and feet, convulsive grinding of the teeth, incoherent mumblings. All these signs seemed to suggest that the sleeper might be having a dream. But how to find out for sure? The obvious answer was to wake up the sleeper and ask him. This is precisely what the University of Chicago team did, and in a very high percentage of awakenings during REM periods, they found the sleeper was indeed dreaming.

The early experiments produced some bizarre experiences. At first, the researchers asked their awakened subjects whether they were dreaming. Imagine their surprise to get a reply like: "No, I was awake. . . . I was having lunch with the president. Not the President of the United States, the president of the college. . . . That is, we were watching a stock-market ticker together, and orange streamers came out of the machine. They all turned into confetti. . . ." Apparently the awakened dreamer was so disoriented that he did not know whether he was dreaming or not. How then to interpret the result if an awakened sleeper simply answered, "No, I wasn't," and turned over and went back to sleep? That problem was soon solved by rephrasing the standard question to, "Was anything going through your mind?"

Members of the Chicago team begged and bribed friends and acquaintances to come and spend some nights in the sleep lab. Night after night they observed these volunteers as they slept, wired to the EEG machine. Time after time they awakened them in various phases of the night's sleep, both during REM periods and during the other sleep stages. Gradually they compiled their statistics. In more than 80 percent of the awakenings during REM periods, the sleepers reported descriptions of dreams. In other phases of sleep, particularly in the deepest phases, dreams were very rarely reported. After the Chicago team reported their results, researchers in other sleep laboratories throughout the world began to check them in their own experiments; their findings were basically the same.

Attention was now eagerly focused on the REM periods of sleep. Researchers discovered that although they follow a fairly regular cycle through the night, the first REM episode is generally the shortest, about five or ten minutes. As the night goes on, the REM periods grow progressively longer, the last episode lasting half an hour or more. It is more difficult to awaken a sleeper during the early REM periods than during the later ones, and the dreams he relates are usually less vivid and detailed than the dreams of early morning. The REM dreams, however, are far more vivid as a rule than the few dreams related after awakenings during other phases of sleep. The dreams of stage 1 and 2 sleep are often more like vague and disconnected thoughts, while the dreams of stage 4 sleep are mainly factual and unemotional, frequently relating to the events of the sleep laboratory. It is difficult to arouse the sleeper during the first REM period of the night, and he is likely to drop back to sleep in the middle of his narrative, leaving the frustrated researcher with only half a dream. Later, closer to the waking time, the sleeper is easier to awaken, and his dream narrations are long and involved.

As the fascinating story of human dream life unfolded, sleep researchers had opportunities to prove or disprove many commonly held beliefs about sleep and dreaming. Have you ever heard, for example, that the events of a dream occur in a flash, that the happenings of many hours in "dream time" may be telescoped into a few seconds of "real time"? The experiments of Kleitman's group indicate that this is not true at all. These researchers tried awakening sleepers after various times of REM sleep, then recording the dreams they narrated. In each case, the events related in the dream story corresponded quite well to the amount of time—say, five, ten, or twenty minutes—that had gone by from the moment when the REMs were first observed until the dreamer was awakened.

Another common myth about dreaming is that most people dream in black and white, while only very creative people dream in color. (A variation is that certain foods cause people to dream in color.) Sleep researchers have found, on the contrary, that people generally dream in color all the time. It may not occur to them to mention this while they are relating the dream, and if they are questioned about the matter on the following day, they may not be able to recall whether the dream was in black and white or color. But if the dreamer is questioned specifically about the colors of objects in his dreams while he is first relating them, he will usually name particular colors quite promptly.

What about the old saying that eating certain foods right before bedtime will cause a person to have more dreams than normal? In the light of modern findings that just about everyone dreams a number of times each night, this does not seem very likely. But a mild case of indigestion might be enough to rouse a

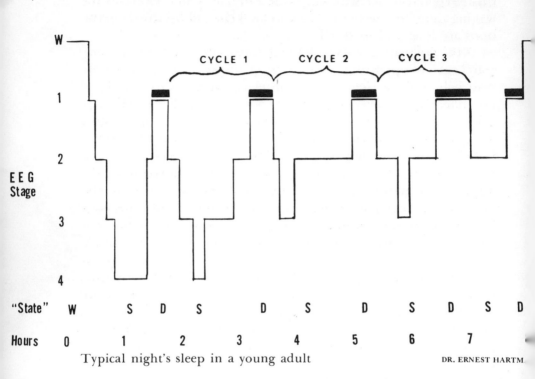

Eye Movements

XX X   XX XX   X XX   XXXX   XX

W

CYCLE 1   CYCLE 2   CYCLE 3

1

2

E E G Stage

3

4

"State"   W   S   D   S   D   S   D   S   D   S   D

Hours   0   1   2   3   4   5   6   7

Typical night's sleep in a young adult   DR. ERNEST HARTM

sleeper during some of the dreams that he would normally sleep through, and thus he might be more likely to remember them in the morning.

Indeed, why don't we remember more of our dreams? After a night with four or five or even six separate mental excursions, we are usually lucky to emerge with any clear recollection of even one—the last dream we had before we awoke. What happened to the other dreams?

Sleep researchers have tried awakening sleepers both during REM periods and at various times after them. These studies have revealed that normally the memory of dreams fades very quickly. Awakening a sleeper during or immediately after a REM episode will usually yield a vividly detailed narrative. But if he is awakened only a few minutes after a REM period ends, although he will probably say he recalls dreaming, his narration will be much less detailed, and only fragments of dreams may be remembered. The usual limit for remembering dreams if the sleeper is allowed to lapse undisturbed from his REM period into a quieter stage of sleep seems to be about eight minutes.

The speed of awakening also seems to have an effect on how much of a dream is recalled. When a dreamer is awakened rapidly, his dream memories are crisp and detailed. If he is allowed to come to himself slowly, his descriptions will more likely be vague and thought-like. You may have noticed that on weekdays, when your sleep is rudely shattered by the raucous buzzing of an alarm clock, you awaken with a vivid memory of a dream. On weekends, when you can drift more slowly into awareness, you may have no recollection of dreaming at all.

There is a simple explanation for the fact that a slow awakening seems to dissipate the memory of dreams. Scientists who study how the brain works have discovered that there are two kinds of memories, short-term and long-term. The short-term memory serves as a sort of temporary storage for facts that were just learned. These are ultimately sorted out and either discarded or filed away in the long-term memory. The sorting-out process is determined by many things. Repetition can help to fix a fact in your long-term memory. When you memorize a song or a poem, you usually repeat it over a few times. Association is another key to long-term memory storage. Many memory-improvement systems work on this basis. In learning a list of words or abbreviations, you might make up a sentence or phrase linking them together. Years ago, for example, schoolchildren were taught to use the phrase "my dear Aunt Sally" to recall the proper order for mathematical manipulations (*m*ultiply, *d*ivide, *a*dd, *s*ubtract). A more straightforward association occurs when you link the name of a new acquaintance with his face. Associations also provide a key for retrieving facts from your "memory bank." Some scientists believe that once a fact is committed to the brain's long-term memory storage, it remains there until the person dies, apparently forgotten but ready to be recalled by the stimulus of the proper association.

Items that the brain does not consider important tend to be discarded, rather than being transferred from the short-term to the long-term memory. Distractions can short-circuit the process. Have you ever looked up an unfamiliar telephone number and dialed it, only to get a busy signal? Before you got a chance to dial again, someone asked you a question. You turned to the telephone again and suddenly realized that you had completely forgotten the number, even though you looked it up just minutes ago. Yet if you had taken the time to repeat the number several times before the distraction, or had formed some association with it (perhaps you might have noticed that some of the numbers formed a familiar pattern, such as 2468), then you might still have recalled it.

Sleep researchers believe that this is what happens to our memory of dreams. If a person is awakened suddenly in the midst of a dream or immediately after it has ended, either by a sleep experimenter or by an alarm clock, or perhaps by an ache or pain in the middle of the night, his mind may focus sharply on the content of the dream, repeat parts of it or form associations, and fix it firmly in the memory. But if the person awakens slowly or sleeps on after the dream is over, other distracting thoughts may blur the dream memory and finally cause it to fade away, to be lost forever.

The difference in speed of awakening may be a partial explanation for the fact that sleepers usually have some difficulty in recalling clearly their early REM dreams of the night, and rarely recall dreaming in the deep phases of stage 3 and stage 4 sleep. These are the times when sleepers are most difficult to arouse. There is evidence to indicate that some mental activity does go on in these "quiet" phases of sleep, however.

There are recurrent nightmares, for example, which are often referred to as night terrors. They are one of the most intensely terrifying experiences that a human being can experience. Often the night terror is a reenactment of a frightening experience that has occurred in real life. A bus driver, for example, accidentally runs over a little girl with his bus. For many nights afterward, in his mind he is back in the grip of that horrible moment, clutching the steering wheel, stamping on the brake, helplessly watching the bus hurtle forward. After the first reports on REM dreaming appeared, sleep researchers naturally expected to find that these night terrors occur during REM episodes. A group of sleep researchers at Mount Sinai Hospital in New York, headed by Charles Fisher, advertised for volunteer subjects who were regularly troubled by these night terrors. Thirty persons who had been suffering from nightmares for years were recruited. But the researchers quickly found to their dismay that most of the subjects had very few nightmares in the laboratory. In the first fifty nights of dream collecting, they totaled only eight nightmares. The scientists theorized that the surprising number of "cures" resulted from the safe atmosphere of the laboratory. A person might not be so likely to become terrified during sleep when he knew that a team of scientists was right there in the next room, watching his every brain wave.

Eventually a good sample of nightmares was collected, and it was discovered that they characteristically do not occur in the REM periods of sleep at all. They occur in stage 4 sleep, which had been assumed to be the deepest and most restful. In the grip of a night terror, a subject may leap out of bed, screaming. He may try to run or even to climb out the laboratory window. But if he is awakened, it is likely that he may not recall anything at all.

Other strange things may happen during the apparent quiet of stage 4 sleep. This is the time when bed-wetting may occur, and it is the time when a sleepwalker may leave his bed, bound on some mysterious errand of which he may have no recollection if he is awakened.

Though the awareness is growing that the non-REM stages of sleep may hold some fascinating riddles to be explored, the main attention of sleep researchers is still focused on the mysteries of

The Never-Never Land, an engraving by Brueghel, is a sixteenth-century interpretation of the world of sleep and dreams.

REM sleep and dreaming. Gradually scientists are finding answers to the questions of why we dream, where the matter of dreams comes from, and what dreams may mean.

One of the first questions that the University of Chicago group explored after REM periods were shown to be linked with dreaming was: what is the significance of the rapid eye movements? Is the dreamer really watching the action of his dream, as he seems to be?

William Dement made a careful analysis of the electrical records of REM periods just before awakening and compared them with the dreams that the sleepers related. In each case, he and his associates tried to guess the probable directions of the subject's eye movements in the dream and found a remarkable correspondence to the EEG tracings. In particular, they noticed that eye movements usually went from side to side. In the few instances in which up-and-down movements were recorded, the dreamer usually related an activity that would account quite plausibly for the eye movements. For example, one dreamer described watching a balloon ascend into the air. In another, in which five separate upward movements were recorded, the dreamer mentioned that she had climbed five steps in her dream.

In addition, the research team scored the EEG records of various dreams as "active" or "passive," according to the numbers of rapid eye movements recorded. Then they went over the narratives of the corresponding dreams and rated them "active" or "passive," according to their content. A dream in which the sleeper was chopping wood or playing tennis, for example, would be considered active, while a dream of eating dinner with a friend or taking an examination in school would be passive. Again a striking correspondence was obtained—the active dreams usually had active EEG records, while the passive dreams had EEG tracings with a relatively small number of rapid eye movements.

Other dream researchers were quick to point out that these correlations were somewhat subjective. Dement and his associates expected to find a correlation, and their unconscious bias might have caused them unwittingly to slant the numerous questionable cases so that the results would fit the theory. Ian Oswald, working at Edinburgh, reports that he was particularly skeptical, and decided to try an independent verification. An associate, Ralph Berger, conducted a series of sleep experiments. Oswald did not come to the lab on those nights, and so was not present when the EEG recordings were being made. Taking the reports of dreams related by the awakened sleepers, he scored them as active or passive according to his impressions of their content. Then, separately, he rated the EEG tracings (labeled in a special code so that he did not know which went with which dreams). Again, excellent agreement was obtained.

Another way to test the hypothesis occurred to Oswald. If REMs really did correspond to the tracking of visual images during dreams, then people born blind, who had never seen images, would not have rapid eye movements during their dreams. But if the REMs were merely a coincidence and did not really follow dream action, then blind people would have REMs during their dreams just like everyone else.

It was not easy to find blind volunteers willing to go off with a strange doctor and sleep in the mental hospital where Oswald had his laboratory. But he did eventually find eight. Three of the men had been blind for relatively short times—for three, ten, and fifteen years. These men said that they could still picture things in their minds by day. EEG tracings of their sleep patterns showed regular patterns of REMs very similar to the sleep patterns of people with normal vision. Three other men had been born blind. Their eyeballs moved freely in their sockets, but they had never had the experience of looking at things in the waking world. To his surprise, Oswald discovered that these men did not have any rapid eye movements during their sleep at all. There were periods, at just the expected regular intervals through the night, when all the other EEG tracings showed the signs typical of REM sleep. Awakened from these periods, the blind men described dreams. (The dream experiences that they described, of course, were sensations of hearing, touching, smelling, and tasting, rather than visual images.) But no REMs. The other two men in the study had been blind since early childhood (more than thirty years before). They said that they no longer saw mental images, and their dreams, too, were not accompanied by REMs.

All these findings would seem to support clearly the idea that the rapid eye movements during dreaming sleep actually follow the action of the dream. But there is some evidence on the other side, as well.

Some scientists point out that REMs are often far too rapid and frantic to correspond to any normal activities. Perhaps, they suggest, only some of the rapid eye movements observed during sleep follow dream action, while the others are due to some other cause that is not related to the content of the dreams.

Moreover, REMs are observed in very young babies, even newborn infants. (Remember that it was in observations of young babies that the true significance of REM periods was first suspected.) Indeed, newborn infants spend about half of their total sleep time in REM sleep, compared with less than a quarter in adults. Since babies at this age sleep about fourteen hours a day, and adults average only about eight, a newborn infant spends nearly four times as many hours a day in REM sleep as an adult.

It would be difficult to imagine that a newborn baby could have stored up enough visual experiences to provide material for all this dreaming time. Thus, it does not seem likely that a sleeping baby's rapid eye movements are following dream action.

Nathaniel Kleitman points out that this evidence does not necessarily refute his theory. After all, babies are born able to make noises, and only later do they learn to modify this ability so as to speak words. Some sleep researchers believe that the rapid eye movements in an infant's sleep are a sort of training for the baby's eyes and nervous system, developing the skills and connections that will be needed to learn to focus the eyes on real objects in the waking world.

Where does the material for dreams come from? Can things that happen while you are sleeping influence what you dream about? If you happen to kick off the covers on a cold night, for example, will this cause you to dream that you are leading an expedition to the North Pole? Your own experiences will probably suggest some answers to these questions. If you have ever been awakened by a thunderstorm, you know that your brain somehow retains some awareness of its surroundings while you are asleep. This awareness can be highly selective. When awake, you are able to filter out the noise of a television set when you are concentrating on your homework, and if your mother calls you when you are in the middle of an interesting activity, you may be able to tell her later quite truthfully that you did not hear her. In the same way, the sleeping brain can tune out sounds that it does not consider important, while still remaining alert to certain key stimuli. A mother, for example, can sleep blissfully through a crashing thunderstorm, but awaken instantly at a small cry from her baby. Some of the sounds and other stimuli that the sleeping brain allows to filter through may be incorporated into dreams. Did you ever awaken from a dream in which you heard a telephone or doorbell ringing, and then discover it was your alarm clock? Experiences much like this are a common occurrence in sleep laboratories. In one case, in fact, the awakened dreamer described himself as standing in the house when he heard the doorbell ring. Someone asked him to answer it. He hesitated for a moment, and as he turned toward the door, the bell rang again. It turned out that the experimenter's finger had slipped while he was ringing the bell to awaken the dreamer, and the bell actually rang two separate times. Later the sleeper was asked to act out the events he had related. It was found that about three seconds elapsed between the two ringings of the dream doorbell, and this was just the time that passed in the laboratory between the first and second soundings of the awakening bell.

Sigmund Freud tried an experiment in which he ate anchovies just before going to bed, to see whether the thirst he would feel during the night would affect his dreams. Sure enough, when he awoke, he was in the midst of a dream of drinking down great gulps of water to quench his thirst. But the only dream that Freud had available to him was the last one before he awoke. Modern sleep researchers can test the effects of stimuli from the outside world on all the dreams of the night.

The twentieth-century artist Soyer gives his interpretation of a dream, called *A Walk in the Sky*.

PRINCETON UNIVERSITY

William Dement and Edward Wolpert conducted a series of studies of this kind. When they sprayed their sleeping subjects with water or sounded noises, about a quarter of the dreams that they recorded seemed to incorporate the real experience into the dream. About a third of their subjects given salty or spicy foods to make them thirsty reported dreams involving drinking.

At New York University, Edwin Bokert went a step farther. He kept his volunteers from eating or drinking for eight hours before the study, then gave them a spicy meal when they arrived at the laboratory. As an added touch, while they slept a tape recording murmured, "a cool delicious drink of water." Many dreams of drinking were recorded. Interestingly, the subjects who successfully quenched their thirst in their dreams did not seem as thirsty when they awoke in the morning as those who had dreams in which they tried to drink but were frustrated. This experiment thus seems to give a bit of support to Freud's theory that dreams serve the function of wish fulfillments.

For a number of years, Calvin Hall, at the Dream Research Institute of Miami, Florida, has been compiling a sort of dream catalogue. Analyzing the records of more than thirty thousand dream narrations, Hall's group is trying to determine the general types of dream content that are typical of various groups of people— normal college students, the aged, people with various physical ailments, and people of different ethnic groups. It is found that most dreams occur in familiar settings—a third in houses; a quarter on means of transportation, such as trains, cars, and planes; a tenth in social situations; a tenth out of doors, and so forth. Family members and friends often are dream characters; sometimes a person who has not been seen for years may figure in a dream; other dream characters seem to be unknown to the dreamer. (Followers of Freud would say that these are really familiar persons in disguise, because their true identity might cause feelings of guilt or anxiety to the sleeper.)

Hall's content analyses have revealed that men tend to dream more about other men than they do about women, while women seem to dream equally often about both sexes. Women's monthly cycle seems to influence their dreams. Just before menstruation, women often have dreams of waiting, while during the first days of the menstrual period, they may have dreams of destruction.

Freud saw many of the symbols of dreams as symbols of the sex organs and sex drives. Because the waking world does not allow sexual drives to be expressed freely, they are expressed as wish fulfillments in dreams; but the brain, to avoid creating feelings of anxiety, censors these expressions and disguises them in symbolic form. Yet Calvin Hall points out that the same dreamer will often have a symbolic dream one night and an openly sexual dream another night. If a "censor" is operating, why does it not operate all the time?

A curious discovery about REM sleep might seem to support Freud's theories. Sleep researchers soon found that their male subjects tended to have erections of the penis periodically during the night. Research teams at the University of Florida and at Mount Sinai Hospital in New York City have both established cycles of penile erections that precisely match the REM cycles. An obvious conclusion would be that these erections correspond to dreams of sexual arousal. But an analysis of the content of the dreams accompanying them indicates only a small fraction of them are clearly sexual dreams. And many of the dreams seem to have no particular sexual content, even symbolically. Moreover, the nightly cycles of penile erections occur not only in young adult men, but also in infants and in extremely old men, as well as in dogs, shrews, and various other members of the animal kingdom. The latest theory explaining the cycle of penile erections that accompanies dreams in men is that the changes in the brain that occur during REM sleep stimulate a region of the brain called the hypothalamus, which contains a special sex center. As REM-sleep activity in the brain dies down, so does the stimulation of this center in the hypothalamus, and the signs of apparent sexual stimulation disappear.

The mind has a whole lifetime of content to draw upon in constructing dream fantasies, but, curiously, the substance of dreams seems to draw heavily on the events of the preceding day. This is a commonplace observation, and there is much experimental evidence to support it.

In one series of studies, David Foulkes and Allan Rechtschaffen showed a group of volunteers films of two popular television shows just before bedtime. One was a Western, with a number of scenes of brutal violence. The other was a romantic comedy. Only rarely were actual elements of the stories incorporated into the night's dreams, but the dreams following the violent Western were much more vivid, imaginative, and intense than the dreams related by subjects who had viewed the comedy.

At the Downstate Medical Center in Brooklyn, New York, a similar technique has been used, but the selection of bedtime films is far more extreme. The assortment includes horrifying documentaries of automobile accidents and a sequence showing the birth of a baby in full detail, along with other films presenting innocuous travelogues. After watching stressful films, the volunteers often took longer to fall asleep than usual and began their REM periods earlier. Yet often, when awakened, they were unable to recall any dreams. The sleep researchers interpret this finding as an indication of repression, caused by the powerful emotional impact of the bedtime films. Among the subjects who did report dreams, some references to the film material were obtained, along with other instances in which elements of the film were apparently cloaked in symbolism.

In one recent experiment to test the theory that dream content is drawn largely from the events of the day, the subjects spent the entire waking day wearing special colored goggles, which filtered out blues and greens and made them see the world in shades of orange-red. During the night, when sleepers were asked to describe the colors of objects in their dreams, the most frequent colors they named were orange and red.

From the results of experiments such as these, Irwin Feinberg of Langley Porter Neuropsychiatric Institute in San Francisco has put together a hypothesis on the function of REM sleep and dreaming. He speculates that during this phase of sleep in particular, the brain sorts out the events of the day and stores away the facts that it considers important in the long-term memory banks. There is an intriguing corroboration of this hypothesis. Sleep scientists have found that the total amount of sleep drops rapidly during childhood, then reaches a plateau in the twenties; remaining at about the same level through the thirties and forties, the total sleep time again declines through old age. Normally the rate of learning new information follows exactly the same sort of curve.

What about the ideas of the ancients, that dreams could foretell the future? Precognition, a knowledge of the future, and various other psychic phenomena have been regaining some degree of scientific respectability in recent years, since the experiments of J. B. Rhine on ESP (extrasensory perception) at Duke University. Many reported instances of ESP have involved experiences during sleep and dreams. Now experiments are under way at Maimonides Hospital in Brooklyn to test these phenomena under scientifically controlled conditions.

In one series of studies, an agent sits in a room in another building and looks at a reproduction of a famous painting. He tries to project his thoughts to a subject sound asleep in the soundproof bedroom of the dream lab. The subject's dreams are recorded, and then an independent judge determines the correspondence of the dream content to the painting viewed by the agent. A surprising number of "hits" has been obtained, some of them extremely vivid and detailed. In one case, when the painting was Van Gogh's "Boats on the Beach," the subject described being on a boardwalk or beach at the seacoast, and mentioned that the scene "makes me think of Van Gogh." The results are even more striking if the target picture is reinforced by music, odors, or appropriate objects. In one instance, the agent concentrated on a painting of a Japanese man with an umbrella, caught in a downpour of rain, and supported the image of the picture with a toy Japanese umbrella. The subject, a man, dreamed of fountains and rain. Tabulations of dream content show that only about one in a hundred dreams by men deal with rain. The results of the dream experiment thus seem strongly to suggest some sort of transfer of thought.

In addition to studies of mental telepathy such as the one described, other experiments at the Maimonides Dream Lab deal with precognition (a subject tries to dream of a painting that a member of the team will pick out the *following day*) and clairvoyance (the subject tries to dream of a picture inside a sealed envelope). The analysis of dreams has come full circle. Sleep researchers of today are using modern scientific techniques to pursue some of the same quests that intrigued the earliest men.

SIX
What Makes Us Sleep

You are reading a book now. Your mind is alert, absorbing new concepts, relating them to past experiences. You may feel as though you could go on forever. Yet some time tonight, waves of tiredness will sweep over you. If you are doing something interesting, you may resist them successfully for a while. But eventually you will go to bed, and, with surprising swiftness, you will lose your awareness of the room about you. You will be asleep.

What is sleep, and what causes it? Is it merely a wasteful interruption of the day's activities, which we might hope some day to eliminate or at least minimize, once we learn enough about the how and why of sleep? Or is sleep the natural state of the body, and wakefulness the interruption? How is sleep produced, and what makes us wake up? What functions does sleep serve for the body?

Men have wondered about these questions since the beginning of time, and many fanciful explanations have been devised. The primitives thought that sleep freed the soul from the body so that it could wander about in the world of the night. (Woe betide the sleeper if his soul happened to be caught and detained in its wanderings!) The ancient Greek physician Alcmeon had a more scientific-sounding explanation. He theorized that a person goes to sleep because his blood flows out of his organs and pools in his veins. When the blood flows back again to its proper place, he wakes up.

Today scientists know more about the workings of the body than the ancient Greeks did. And so it is natural for modern sleep researchers to seek answers to the how and why of sleep in the brain, the master control center of the body.

The two large halves, or hemispheres, of the brain are perched at the top of the spinal cord, looking something like two halves of a grapefruit balanced on the end of a banana. At the top of the spinal cord (the end of the banana) is a structure called the brainstem. The lowest portion of the brainstem, just above the end of the spinal cord, is called the medulla. In it are found important control centers that govern such vital functions of the body as breathing and swallowing. Moving upward, the next region of the brainstem is called the pons, and just above it is the hypothalamus. Neurologists have developed extremely fine techniques of implanting wire electrodes into very specific regions of the brains of animals. Using such techniques, they have discovered a number of different control regions in the hypothalamus. When one of these is stimulated with an electric current, the animal will immediately go to its water dispenser and drink as though it were desperately thirsty. This is the thirst center. In other regions of the hypothalamus, scientists have discovered a hunger center, which prompts an animal to eat; a satiety center, which makes the animal stop eating as though it has had its fill; a fear center, which when stimulated will make a cat cringe in terror at the sight of a mouse; an anger center; and even a pleasure center, the stimulation of which seems to bring sensations of intense delight.

Another region of the brain, which forms a sort of lump to the

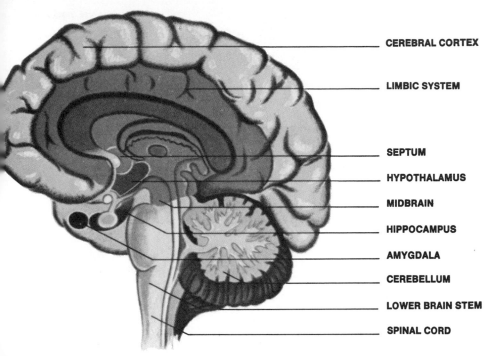

CEREBRAL CORTEX

LIMBIC SYSTEM

SEPTUM

HYPOTHALAMUS

MIDBRAIN

HIPPOCAMPUS

AMYGDALA

CEREBELLUM

LOWER BRAIN STEM

SPINAL CORD

The brain and its important components

rear of the brainstem, is the cerebellum. The bony projection of your skull that you can feel if you run your hand along the back of your head helps to protect the cerebellum from injury. The cerebellum's function is to coordinate muscle activities. You would not be able to throw a baseball accurately or thread a needle without an efficiently working cerebellum.

The two large hemispheres, which would correspond to the halves of the grapefruit, form the cerebrum, the thinking part of the brain. This part of the brain receives and analyzes messages from the eyes, ears, and other sense organs, and sends out messages to control the actions of the muscles. Thoughts and plans are formed in the cerebrum, and memories are stored here. Nearly all this activity occurs in the cerebral cortex, the thin, wrinkled outer layer of the cerebrum (like the peel of the grapefruit, only much thinner). Each part of the cerebral cortex has its own function—there are sensory zones, speech-association zones, motor zones, and so forth. Neurologists have succeeded in drawing up detailed maps of the cerebral cortex by stimulating individual nerve cells and groups of cells with minute electric currents, and by studying the effects of accidents that destroyed parts of the brain.

Studies of brain damage have provided important clues to the brain systems that control sleeping and waking. Brain surgeons noticed early that large areas of the cerebrum could be damaged without causing the victim to lose consciousness. Yet when very small regions of the brainstem were only slightly damaged, the patients were usually unconscious. More evidence came from a fatal disease called sleeping sickness. This disease gets its name from its most obvious symptom: its victims are overwhelmed by sleepiness, and just before death it is almost impossible to rouse them. Autopsies of these victims revealed an inflammation of the brain—not of the cerebrum, but of the brainstem.

With this background, it seemed very likely that some sort of sleep control center must be located in the brainstem. And since so many control centers had already been found in the hypothalamus, that seemed a likely place to look.

Evidence of sleep control centers in the hypothalamus was first discovered by a Swiss physiologist, Walter Hess, during the 1930s and '40s. He was the same researcher who had discovered the other control centers in the hypothalamus, in studies begun in the 1920s. Now, stimulating new regions of the hypothalamus, he found first a region that could cause a sleeping animal to wake up, and then a region that could be stimulated to put a waking animal to sleep.

During the years that followed, other scientists discovered new "wake-up" centers in various parts of the brainstem. It was eventually realized that there was a whole network extending through the brainstem, from the spinal cord up to the hypothalamus. This network was named the *reticular* (or netlike) *activating system* (RAS), and it was found to have numerous nerve connections to virtually every part of the cerebral cortex. If these nerve connections were cut, the animal promptly fell into a deep sleep, and no stimulus could wake it. It did not die, it simply slept on, endlessly.

It seemed evident that this reticular activating system must send messages to the cortex to keep it alert. In the late 1940s, this theory was corroborated. Experimenters implanted tiny wire electrodes in the brains of cats and monkeys. One set of electrodes, inserted in the cortex, provided an EEG record of the animals' brain waves. (The animals recovered quickly from the operation and did not seem to be bothered either by the electrodes or by the fine cables that linked them to the EEG machine.) Another set of electrodes was inserted into the reticular activating system in the brainstem. When an animal fell asleep, a small electric current was passed into the brainstem. Immediately the animal awoke.

Further experiments with implanted electrodes and delicate operations on the brain, selectively cutting certain nerve connections while leaving others intact, gradually built up a coherent picture of what wakes us up and keeps us awake. All the sense organs send messages to the cerebral cortex, but at the same time they have additional pathways that carry messages to the reticular activating system. Everything you see and hear and taste and smell and touch is not only perceived and analyzed in the cortex, but also helps to keep your RAS in a seething state of excitement. An excited RAS continually sends out messages of its own, both upward to the cortex and downward to the spinal cord. The higher brain and spinal cord are both kept in a state of keen alertness, enabling them to cope efficiently with any problems that might arise. An alerted cortex can perceive and analyze incoming messages from the sense organs, determine their importance, and decide on appropriate action. The spinal cord, stimulated by the RAS, keeps the muscles toned up and ready to carry out any actions the brain may order. Messages coming back to the RAS from the cortex and various parts of the body help to stimulate the RAS, which in turn sends out its own messages to stimulate the cortex and spinal cord, and so on in a circle.

Have you ever lain awake at night worrying about something? The more you worried, the more messages your cortex sent down to your RAS, stimulating it to send its own messages back to stimulate the cortex so that you could worry even more efficiently. Back and forth the messages flew, like a dog chasing its tail, and you stayed wide-awake.

The discovery of the reticular activating system seemed to take care of the question of what wakes people up and keeps them awake. But that still left the problem of what makes people sleep. It seems obvious that something must turn down the RAS every night; otherwise we would never get to sleep. But what is it?

The mechanisms that control sleep are still being explored. Sleep researchers have obtained enough evidence to work out some plausible ideas, but the exact details are not yet completely clear.

In attempting to find out how the brain's sleep-controlling systems work, modern scientists have turned away from the idea of stimulating nerve cells and toward a new technique that is closer to the natural way the brain works, through the effects of chemicals. Using tiny, hollow guide tubes that can be inserted into the brain like an electrode, a layer of cells can be touched by a single microcrystal of a pure chemical. Raul Hernandez-Peon, a neurophysiologist working in Mexico City, discovered that a natural brain chemical called acetylcholine, injected into various regions of the brainstem, could put a cat to sleep. How fast the cat fell asleep depended on where the chemical was injected: in one region of the hypothalamus, acetylcholine produced sleep within two to five minutes; when applied to another point, the chemical put the animal to sleep within seconds. The effect was so rapid that if the cat happened to be eating at the time, its head dropped right into the feeding dish.

Another natural chemical, adrenalin, applied at the same spots where acetylcholine induced sleep, caused sleeping animals to wake up.

Evidence is accumulating to indicate that still another natural brain chemical, serotonin, is involved in putting us to sleep. The level of this chemical in the brain has been shown to rise and fall rhythmically, every twenty-four hours. In numerous experiments on cats, in which various parts of the brain were selectively destroyed, Michel Jouvet, a French physiologist working in Lyons, discovered a key group of structures in the brainstem called the nuclei of raphe. The raphe system manufactures serotonin; if it is destroyed, the cat does not sleep. Injection of drugs that cause a suppression of the serotonin in the brain produces the same effect. Injections of serotonin, on the other hand, or of other chemicals that are known to be changed into serotonin in the brain, will produce a state of slow-wave sleep.

In addition to the raphe system, Jouvet has found another center in the brainstem, the locus coeruleus. This center produces REM sleep, and it seems to work by means of noradrenalin. Jouvet suggests that these two systems work in a cyclic fashion to slow down the reticular activating system and bring about the two phases of sleep.

Research continues. There are enzymes in the brain that act to break down chemicals called monoamines (both serotonin and adrenalin belong to the class of monoamines). These enzymes are called monoamine oxidases, and drugs have been discovered that inhibit their function (monoamine oxidase inhibitors). If the functions of monoamine oxidase are inhibited, the levels of the brain monoamines would be expected to build up. And if serotonin and adrenalin really are associated with the natural mechanisms of sleep, monoamine oxidase inhibitors should have a very pronounced effect on sleep.

This is indeed the case. In experiments on cats, Jouvet found that injections of a monoamine oxidase inhibitor eliminated REM sleep. Neither slow-wave sleep nor wakefulness seemed to be affected. Other monoamine oxidase inhibitors have been used on humans. They were not really prescribed for sleep disorders.

Cats are good sleepers—at home, in the lab, almost anywhere.

FREDERICK J. BREDA

These drugs have been found to be powerful "psychic energizers," which can restore feelings of well-being and good spirits to people who have been locked in deep depressions for months or even years. Many patients with severe depression suffer from insomnia as well, unable to fall asleep at night or waking too early in the morning.

In a study at Rockland State Hospital in New York, Nathan Kline prescribed monoamine oxidase inhibitors for some of his patients. Within about two weeks, the patients were feeling cheerful and energetic. Yet their insomnia had not been helped; if anything, they were sleeping less than ever, although they did not seem to be showing any ill effects. Curious, Kline himself tried the drug, and for two months he found himself sleeping only three hours a night and feeling fine. Caution finally prompted him to stop taking the drug, as the long-term effects of such a radical change in sleeping habits were unknown.

It was a wise decision. The widespread use of monoamine oxidase inhibitors soon revealed some dangerous side effects. Many natural foods—particularly cheeses, chocolates, and liver—are rich in amines. These are normally broken down by monoamine oxidases in the body. But if these key enzymes are blocked, the amines can build up and poison various body systems, causing blinding headaches and even, in some extreme cases, heart attacks or strokes.

Some sleep researchers are searching for natural "hypnotoxins," chemicals that might build up in the waking body and ultimately trigger sleep. In 1967, a research team at Harvard University reported that carefully filtered cerebrospinal fluid from goats that had been kept awake for seventy-two hours produced sleep in both cats and rats when it was injected into their brains. The effect on rats was particularly striking. Rats are normally nocturnal animals, which are active at night and nap during most of the day. If the experimental rats were injected with cerebrospinal fluid from sleep-deprived goats at 9 P.M., they tended to shift their normal routine. During the night that followed, instead of moving about actively, they curled up to sleep in their cages, waking only occasionally for food and water. If they were handled, they awakened normally, but they went back to sleep as soon as they were left alone. The effects of the injection wore off within about twenty-four hours. Injections of cerebrospinal fluid from goats that had been allowed to sleep normally did not produce any effect. After their initial success, the team set to work trying to isolate the substance in a purer form, and obtained a product even more effective than the original fluid.

The following year, another sleep chemical was reported by Raul Henandez-Peon, the Mexican researcher who had spent five years working with acetylcholine. Hernandez-Peon extracted a substance from the brains of sleeping cats that quickly induced sleep when it was injected into the brains of alert cats. The sleep induced seemed normal both to outward appearances and according to EEG records. The depth of sleep depended on the state of the cat from which the substance was taken. Fluid taken from a cat sleeping lightly produced drowsiness or relaxation; fluid from a cat in deep sleep induced deep sleep. Hernandez-Peon had expected the sleep inducer to be acetylcholine, but chemical tests showed that it was not; what the chemical might be was still uncertain.

Little by little, bits of the puzzle are fitted in. The picture is not yet complete, but sleep researchers hope that they will ultimately learn enough about the mechanisms of sleep to be able to control them at will—to help people who have difficulty in sleeping, and perhaps one day to make the sleep of normal people more effective.

SEVEN
Without Sleep

Have you ever missed a whole night's sleep? Perhaps you had a project due the next day; for one reason or another, you had put off working on it, but now the deadline could not be delayed. Perhaps you were on a trip, with a flood of new and exciting experiences to keep you too stimulated to sleep. If you have had the experience of staying up all night, you probably noticed some interesting sensations. Waves of tiredness swept over you as you reached your usual sleeptime. But after a while these passed, and you felt strong and mentally keen again. There were periods of confidence and exhilaration—"Who needs sleep, anyway?"—but then there were new waves of fatigue, particularly in the early-morning hours, when your body temperature cycle was touching its twenty-four-hour low. By morning, your usual waking time, you probably felt much better—quite your normal self. But as the day wore on, there were more waves of tiredness. Someone watching you closely might have noticed that there were periods —only a few seconds, perhaps—when you did not seem to be pay-ing attention, would not answer a direct question, or seemed to lose track of the conversation. You were actually taking a tiny nap, a "microsleep" so brief that you yourself may not have been aware of it at all. Other changes may have been apparent to a close observer: perhaps you were a bit irritable and had difficulty concentrating. At last, it was time to go to bed, and if you were lucky enough to be able to sleep as long as you wished, you probably expected to make up the entire eight hours or more that you had missed. Yet you found to your surprise that only a couple of extra hours past your normal waking time, you were up and feeling your normal self again. *However*

The pressures of modern jobs and the wide range of stimulating activities that can be engaged in at any hour of the day or night have made many people wonder whether sleep is really necessary—whether it might be possible to cut it out entirely, or at least reduce this imposition of "lost time." A third of life seems like a lot of time to spend in a state of oblivion.

The EEG machine and other tools and techniques of modern sleep researchers have given them the means to study what happens when people do without sleep. Many experiments have been conducted, both on total sleep deprivation—staying awake for extended periods of time—and on cutting down the total length of sleep or cutting out specific phases of sleep. *→109*

Volunteers have stayed awake for the sake of science, and others have staged extended "walkathons" as publicity campaigns for various charities. In 1959, for example, a New York disc jockey, Peter Tripp, undertook to stay awake continuously for two hundred hours to win publicity for the March of Dimes. Considerable evidence had already accumulated to indicate the dangers of going without sleep for more than eight days straight (one disc jockey, who had previous signs of mental instability, had such pronounced aftereffects from going without sleep for a week that he wound up in a mental institution). But Tripp was determined to have every safeguard. A team of doctors and psychiatrists was available day and night to monitor his condition and give him any aid he might need. He was in top physical condition, and he intended to continue eating an athlete's high-protein diet to maintain his health.

The first problem Peter Tripp encountered, as might be expected, was an overpowering sleepiness. During his regular broadcasts he was fine, but the hours between seemed to stretch on interminably. The batteries of tests each day—EEG, blood and urine analyses, various psychological tests—helped a little to keep him stimulated, and so did walks through the city streets and conversations with friends and people involved in the study. By the third day without sleep, peculiar things began happening. As Tripp changed his shoes, he noticed a cobweb in one of them. The psychiatrist to whom he pointed it out did not see it at all. Specks on the table seemed to be running around like bugs. He was convinced there was a rabbit in the broadcasting booth.

Five days without sleep. Peter Tripp's health still seemed good, and he was handling his broadcasts with ease. But he was having trouble remembering things. He could do only the simplest tests of arithmetic and mental reasoning. He even stumbled on the alphabet. The hallucinations continued. A doctor's tie seemed to be jumping out of place. Furry worms swarmed on another doctor's coat. Tripp began to wonder if people were playing practical jokes on him. He was convinced of this when he opened a bureau drawer and flames seemed to spurt out at him.

The seventh day. The sleepless disc jockey was confused. Sometimes he could not remember who he was or where he was. The face of an actor friend, made up for the role of Dracula, stared down at him from a wall clock. EEG tracings showed the slow waves of deep sleep, even though to all outward appearances Tripp was awake. Yet somehow, at five o'clock each afternoon, he became the old Peter Tripp once more, able to keep up a smooth and witty patter for the full three hours of his broadcast.

On the morning of the last day, there was a crisis. For days now, the idea had been growing within Tripp that the doctors and nurses were united in some terrible conspiracy against him. Now, suddenly, it all became crystal clear. A well-known neurologist had arrived to examine him. The doctor was wearing dark clothes and carried an umbrella, even though the sun was shining brightly. He asked Tripp to undress and lie down on the examining table. Suddenly, lying there with the somber-looking doctor peering down at him, Tripp *knew*—the doctor was really an undertaker who had come to bury him alive! Screaming in terror, he leaped out of the room and fled naked down the corridor.

Somehow Peter Tripp managed to finish the day. After his evening broadcast and an hour-long battery of tests, he went to bed and slept a solid thirteen hours. When he awoke, he was calm and refreshed. The terrors and hallucinations that had tormented him had vanished. Once more he was able to run through tests of memory and mental agility with ease. Somehow, mysteriously, he had been restored by one night's sleep.

Sleep researchers point out that the wide public attention focused on Peter Tripp's attempt to go without sleep probably accentuated the mental aberrations that resulted. And indeed, under the more sedate and controlled conditions of sleep-deprivation experiments in the laboratory, the changes have been much less striking. Yet certain effects have been consistently obtained.

The volunteers are quickly assailed by almost overwhelming waves of fatigue. Sleep researcher Ian Oswald tells of walking two sleep-deprived volunteers around the streets of Edinburgh, and time and time again seeing their eyelids slowly closing even as they walked. Constant diversions and changing stimuli must be provided to keep the subjects awake. Sleep researchers have used word games, visits to stores, pinball machines, and countless other devices to keep volunteers from falling asleep on their feet.

Wilse Webb of the University of Florida makes an interesting point. In experiments on animals, two techniques can be used to produce sleep deprivation. The animal can be given an electric shock or some other punishment every time it lapses into sleep. Or a positive technique can be used, keeping the animal awake by continually changing its environment with new and interesting stimuli. These two techniques produce entirely different sleep responses. Animals who are punished for sleeping with electric shocks fall asleep despite these punishments after about forty-two hours. Yet animals that are kept positively stimulated can be kept awake easily for four or five days.

Another consistent finding of sleep-deprivation experiments on

There are various types of sleep deprivation. Subjects deprived of deep sleep or very deep sleep react differently from those who lose only light sleep. These EEG tracings illustrate the differences in brain waves.

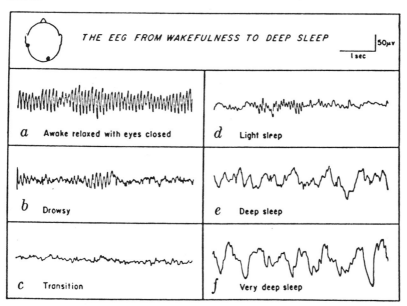

THE EEG FROM WAKEFULNESS TO DEEP SLEEP 50μv 1 sec

a Awoke relaxed with eyes closed

d Light sleep

b Drowsy

e Deep sleep

c Transition

f Very deep sleep

human volunteers has been a growing irritability and other personality changes.) Hallucinations are frequent, and the subject often builds up delusions of persecution—he becomes convinced that the doctors and other members of the research team are plotting against him, playing tricks to make him appear foolish, or even planning to murder him. In many ways the sleep-deprived subject resembles a mental patient, suffering from a severe psychosis.

(Tests of reaction time and mental ability reveal some subtle changes. If the subject is allowed to work at his own speed and correct any mistakes he might make, and the tests are relatively short, no significant changes in ability may be evident. But when questions must be answered at a rapid pace that the subject cannot control, he begins to make many errors. He cannot concentrate his attention on one thing for extended periods. If he is asked to press a buzzer, for example, everytime an X appears on a lighted screen, his performance will be erratic.)Sometimes he will press the buzzer promptly after the X appears, with approximately his usual reaction time. Sometimes there will be a long delay before he presses the buzzer. Sometimes he will miss the X entirely and fail to press the buzzer at all. Sometimes he will give a "false alarm," pressing the buzzer when no X has appeared, as though he suddenly realized that his attention had wandered (in a microsleep, perhaps) and he wanted to make up for it.

Memory failures, wandering of attention, and all-pervading fatigue lead to a general listlessness and inaction. The volunteers quickly give up reading and other activities that require mental effort. As the days without sleep go by, the effort of taking all but the simplest mental tests becomes an agony. They while away the hours watching television or engaging in aimless conversation, sometimes lapsing into unintelligible gibberish or snatches of phrases that seem to relate to some internal waking dream.

(The findings of sleep-deprivation studies may have important practical applications. In military situations, personnel frequently are asked to stand duty for long periods or at irregular intervals, breaking up the normal rhythms of sleep. Imagine the results if a soldier on a battlefield is lost in a microsleep just as an important order is given to him, or a communications officer manning a radar post fails to note a significant "blip" or turns in a false alarm that may result in a missile launch. Air-traffic controllers and physicians are other professionals whose working conditions often interfere with normal sleep patterns, yet impose on them a need for precise skills and split-second decisions that may literally mean life or death for other humans.

What happens during the night's sleep following a long period of sleep deprivation? EEG records show that after a moderate period of sleep deprivation, the subject spends a larger-than-normal fraction of his first night's sleep in the deep sleep of stage 4. He may spend so much time in deep sleep that he gets less than his normal quota of REM sleep. But on the following night, he seems to make up for this by spending an increased time in REM sleep. After very long periods of sleep deprivation, more than two hundred hours, there seems to be an increase in both kinds of sleep, slow-wave and REM sleep. The sleep-starved subject seems to be sleeping more efficiently, spending less time than usual in the lighter stages of sleep.

Except under emergency conditions, such as a major flood or earthquake, examples of complete sleep deprivation for extended periods are rare in the lives of normal people. But examples of partial sleep deprivation are frequent. The college student who studies late into the night for his exams and then must wake up early for classes; the doctor who may be disturbed by an emergency call at any hour of the night; the policeman or industrial worker whose work shifts are rotated every few days so that his body barely has a chance to adjust to the night shift before he is back on the day shift again; the housewife whose young baby wakes up every few hours for feedings—all these and many more do not have an opportunity to get the "solid eight hours a night" that we consider the norm.

A number of studies have already been conducted to determine the effects of partial sleep deprivation. When the night ration of sleep is cut in half, for example, the EEG tracings reveal an unexpected effect. You may recall that in a normal eight-hour night of sleep, most of the deep sleep occurs during the first half of the night, while most of the REM sleep occurs in the second half. If the effect of reducing the sleeping time to four hours a night were simply cutting off the second half of the sleep cycle, the EEG record would be expected to show a close-to-normal amount of deep sleep but a very severe cut in REM sleep. Yet after the subjects have had a chance to adjust to the new sleep schedule for a few nights, the sleep cycles begin to change. Some of the REM sleep "moves up" into the first four hours, so that the proportion of REM sleep to non-REM sleep becomes almost normal. Meanwhile, the proportion of stage 4 sleep increases, at the expense of the lighter stages, so that very little of the normal quota is lost. The body seems to have the ability to adjust to changing conditions to get the kinds of sleep it needs most.

The adjustment is not completely effective, however. This is revealed on the first night the subject is allowed to sleep as long as he wishes. There is a sort of "REM rebound," with a far greater amount of time than usual spent in REM periods. It is as though the sleeper is trying to make up for the REM sleep that he missed over the past days. Curiously, a small stage 4 rebound is also observed, even though the four-hour schedule produced very little deep-sleep deprivation.

What are the effects of limiting sleeping time on a person's waking life? In Cambridge, England, R. T. Wilkinson studied twenty-four volunteers for two-night periods in which they were allowed to sleep for one, two, three, or five hours each night. During the day, he kept them at a battery of tests of arithmetic ability and vigilance (responding properly to signals). Wilkinson found that the subjects' ability to perform on the vigilance tasks did not seem to be affected until sleep time was reduced below three hours. On the other hand, the volunteers' motivation and willingness to cooperate declined after much smaller reductions in sleeping time. Wilkinson points out that down to three hours, the subjects were getting close to their normal quota of stage 4 sleep. But even when sleeping time was cut only to five hours, there was already a substantial deprivation of REM sleep. The sleep researcher believes that stage 4 sleep is related to the ability to perform tasks, while REM sleep is connected with motivation.

This albino rat is on a small pedestal, typical of a water-tank deprivation situation.

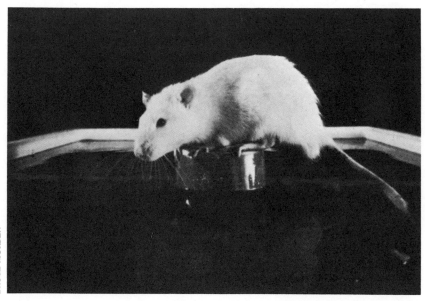

A number of experiments have been designed to test the effects of deprivation of specific stages of sleep, while leaving the total sleeping time basically unchanged.

In one of the landmark experiments, William Dement deprived sleepers of their REM sleep by sounding a buzzer every time their EEG tracings showed that a REM period was about to begin. He found that the sleeper's body fought to catch up on its REM quota. One volunteer, for example, had to be awakened seven times in the first night. On the second night, he made ten different attempts to go into REM sleep, and on the third night, seventeen. By the seventh night, the subject had to be awakened twenty-four separate times to thwart his attempts at REM sleep. When he was allowed at last to sleep undisturbed, he spent a third of his sleeping time in REM periods, nearly twice his normal amount.

Dement noted some personality changes in his REM-deprived volunteers. They became irritable and had difficulty in concentrating. Some developed a persistent hunger or other cravings.

Meanwhile, in Lyons, France, Michel Jouvet was conducting experiments along a similar line with cats. He had devised an ingenious method for depriving the cats of REM sleep without affecting their normal sleep. He placed the cat on a small platform made of bricks in the middle of a pool of water. In its normal curled-up deep-sleep position, the cat was reasonably comfortable. But as soon as a REM period set in, the cat's neck muscles went limp and its head lolled into the water. At this, it promptly woke up. After reading Jouvet's reports, Dement, too, began to experiment on cats. The two researchers were able to keep cats deprived of REM sleep for far longer periods than they would dare to try with humans. After long periods of REM deprivation, some bizarre changes were observed. Some of the cats seemed to be constantly hungry, and prowled incessantly looking for food. Some of the REM-deprived cats seemed to have an increased sex drive. They would even try to mount other male cats, anesthetized cats, and even dead cats—decidedly abnormal behavior for a tom.

Like REM-deprived human volunteers, Jouvet's and Dement's cats showed a typical REM rebound when they were allowed to sleep undisturbed; for several days, they spent up to 60 percent of their sleeping time in REM sleep.

Dement observed that the brain of a REM-deprived cat is unusually excitable, and his team made an unexpected discovery. One day, a member of the team accidentally shocked a REM-deprived animal. In the normal state, the small shock would have had little effect. But the REM-deprived animal went into convulsions. Curiously, a REM-deprived animal that received a shock did not usually show a REM rebound when it was allowed to sleep undisturbed. Yet its brain waves returned to normal all the same. It seemed that in some way, the electric shock discharged some sort of energy that had built up in the brain. Dement believes that this is the function that packets of REM sleep normally serve.

What about stage 4 sleep? Since this is the type of sleep that people tend to make up first after total sleep deprivation, it seems evident that it is essential to the body. What are the effects of depriving just the stage 4 sleep, while leaving the total sleeping time unchanged? Wilse Webb at the University of Florida worked out a way to deprive volunteers of their stage 4 sleep. Every time their EEG tracings showed the slow-wave pattern of deep sleep, he sounded a tone. This stimulus was not enough to wake them, but it nudged the sleepers up into a lighter stage of sleep. The tone was sounded again every time the sleeper tried to descend into stage 4 sleep. On the following night, the volunteers were allowed to sleep undisturbed. As expected, they showed a pronounced stage 4 rebound, making up for the lost quality of their previous night's sleep.

In experiments in which volunteers have been deprived of stage 4 sleep for longer periods, some distinct effects have been observed. The volunteers became listless and depressed. They felt uncomfortable and suffered from vague physical complaints.

These experiments have some important implications for our modern life. It has been shown that when a sleeper is exposed to a loud noise, such as the roar that a jet plane passing overhead might produce, his adrenal glands are activated. Stimulating hormones such as adrenalin and noradrenalin are produced and circulate through his bloodstream. Stage 4 sleep is dissipated, and he stirs restlessly, slipping up into a lighter stage of sleep even though he does not awaken or have any conscious awareness of being disturbed. The noise pollution that pervades our modern world—passing planes, the whirr of air conditioners and other electric motors, the roar of power mowers, jack hammers, and snowmobiles—may be depriving many people of an important fraction of their stage 4 sleep, particularly those who work odd shifts and must try to sleep during the daytime when the rest of the world is up and bustling.

A chronic form of stage 4 deprivation may also contribute to the severe depression and other ills that often accompany old age. Studies of older sleepers have shown that they generally get less total sleep, awaken more often in the middle of the night, and get less stage 4 sleep than teenagers and young adults. A recurrent cough or the ache in a rheumatic joint may be enough to stir an older sleeper out of his restful slow-wave sleep into a lighter stage, or even awaken him entirely. In the middle of the night, when the room is dark and quiet, there are few other stimuli to compete with an ache or pain for attention in the brain, and the sleeper may toss and turn, unable to fall back to sleep. Some light sleepers, in fact, are firmly convinced that they never sleep at all. A series of awakenings during the night merges in their minds, and they do not remember the periods of sleep in between. This has happened numerous times in sleep laboratories, and the indignant insomniac is astonished to be shown a roll of EEG tracings proving that he was indeed asleep.

EIGHT
Remedies for Troubled Sleep

For millions of people, the night is the time of a fierce internal battle, and the bedroom is the battlefield. They lie down tensely in the bed, hoping against hope that tonight some miracle will occur and they will get a good night's sleep, but resignedly expecting the worst. As they lie there rigidly, the ticking of the clock or the blare of a neighbor's television set seems to swell and fill the room. The bed is too hard—or too soft—and the would-be sleeper turns and shifts, trying vainly to find a more comfortable position. Perhaps he switches on the lamp and reads for awhile, trying to lull his mind into relaxation. But the book only seems to stimulate him even more. At last, deep into the night, when he is limp with fatigue and has nearly given up hope, he sinks into a troubled, fitful doze.

This is one form of insomnia, or inability to sleep. In another variation, the insomniac has little trouble falling asleep, but then he wakes, again and again, through the night. Or he may sleep for five hours or so and then awaken, convinced that he will be unable to fall asleep again that night.

The chronic sleep loss of the insomniac can produce depression, irritability, and a persistent sleepiness that threaten to ruin his waking life. It is thus little wonder that many people grasp frantically at any means that offers some promise of relief.

Sleep masks and earplugs are bought by the millions in an effort to shut out distracting stimuli. Mattress salesmen tout the relative merits of their products. Waterbeds are currently enjoying some popularity as the ultimate for nighttime relaxation.

By far the majority of insomniacs look to sleeping pills as the answer to their problem. Antihistamines, drugs that are used to treat allergies and have a mild sleep-producing effect, are sold freely over the counter in drugstores. "Safe and easy, sleep, sleep, sleep," croons the commercial for a mixture of this type.

Barbiturates are stronger sedatives, and they can produce addiction: the user's body becomes dependent upon them, and he is unable to stop taking the drug without serious physical consequences. As a result, these drugs can be obtained only with a prescription; they should be taken under the strict supervision of a doctor. But many doctors prescribe barbiturates and other sleeping pills quite freely, without running any sort of follow-up tests to see how their patients are faring.

Some of the newer tranquilizers and psychic energizers (such as the monoamine oxidase inhibitors) may also be prescribed in an effort to normalize sleeping patterns.

Modern sleep-research techniques have provided experimenters with the means of determining what sleeping pills really accomplish and how they work. The early results of these studies are yielding some disturbing findings. It seems that even drugs that significantly increase total sleeping time produce drastic changes in the quality and rhythm of sleep, changes that may have dangerous consequences for the user.

How would you design an experiment to test the effects of a sleeping pill? You might suggest that after a few nights in the sleep laboratory to establish a baseline—a consistent record of the

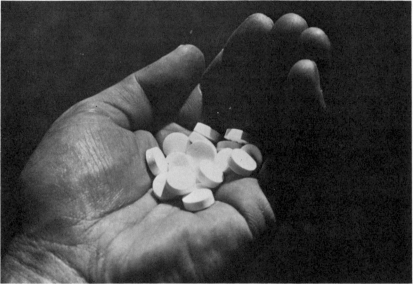

The "easy way out," taking one or more of the various kinds of barbiturates and antihistamines to help induce sleep, can often lead to larger problems of addiction and lethargy.

subject's normal sleeping habits—the volunteer should be given a sleeping pill. A comparison of that night's EEG records with the normal sleeping pattern will reveal the effects of the drug.

Such an experimental design overlooks one important factor. Researchers have found that if a person is given a pill made of sugar or some other innocuous chemical and told that it is a drug that will produce a certain effect, there is an excellent chance that precisely that effect will be observed. The sugar pill could not have produced the effect; it was brought about by the patient's own mind. This effect has long been known to practicing physicians, and they have a special name for the inert pill successfully masquerading as a drug. They call it a placebo, a word meaning "I shall please." At one time, placebos were a respectable part of the medical arsenal, freely prescribed to the patient when the doctor had no better idea of how to treat him. (A placebo could do no harm, it was reasoned, and might well do some good.) Today, physicians prefer to try to ferret out the cause of an ailment and prescribe a drug that produces a specific, proven effect. But the placebo effect is still an important confusing factor in testing new drugs. A patient's faith in the power of a new drug may be so strong that striking results are obtained even though the drug has little true effectiveness. After a while, when the novelty has worn off, doctors are surprised to find that the drug does not seem to be getting results anymore.

Elaborate experimental schemes have been worked out to try to eliminate the placebo effect. One group of patients is given a true placebo, to act as a control, while another group with the same symptoms is given the drug to be tested. The patients do not know which they are getting; sometimes, even the doctor does not know until afterward, when the results of the tests are tabulated and analyzed.

Just such techniques must be used in testing drugs in the sleep laboratory. Typically the subjects will receive a placebo for several nights, then (though they do not realize it) the drug will be

Dr. Ian Oswald, a sleep researcher at the University of Edinburgh, Scotland, is shown here in his lab.

substituted for one or more nights, and finally they receive the placebo again to test the effects of withdrawal of the drug. Even more elaborate schemes of rotation may be used to eliminate as many variable conditions as possible.

Using such techniques, Ian Oswald's group in Edinburgh has discovered that barbiturates, opiates, and some other common sleeping drugs have a profound effect on sleeping patterns. They do help an insomniac get to sleep (or, depending on the drug, keep him from waking up too early). But they produce a substantial decrease in the amount of REM sleep. If the subject continues to take the barbiturate, the effect gradually fades away. His body seems to get accustomed to the drug, to incorporate it into its natural chemistry. But then, what happens if the drug is withdrawn? There is a terrific REM rebound, with an orgy of dreams, many of them violent nightmares.

In one study, two medical students in the middle of their long vacation volunteered for a long-term experiment. First their normal sleep was recorded for five nights. Then, every night for two weeks, they received sleeping pills. At first they complained of hangovers when they awoke each morning. Gradually they got accustomed to the drug, and the hangovers disappeared. The EEG records of the first few nights with the pills showed very little REM sleep, but by the end of two weeks on the drug, the sleep patterns were practically back to normal. Then the sleeping pills were stopped. For a while the volunteers had difficulty getting to sleep at night, and they felt a bit shaky during the day. Their percentage of REM sleep swung far above the normal level, reaching a peak on the third day. Slowly the sleep patterns normalized, and by the end of two weeks without the drug, the subjects were getting their usual amounts of the various stages of sleep again.

These studies have been corroborated by Anthony Kales at UCLA. Kales studied the effects of a number of commonly used sleeping pills and found that only a few, including the long-used chloral hydrate, do not suppress REM sleep. Like Oswald, Kales found an REM rebound when the drugs were withdrawn.

These studies suggest an explanation of how costly and dangerous drug dependences get started. Picture an insomniac who tries sleeping pills. After a few weeks, he finds that he is sleeping a relatively normal time, although perhaps he does not feel quite as well as he had hoped. He thinks that he may be able to do without the pills now, so he stops taking them. On the very first night, he is awakened repeatedly by a series of frightening nightmares. The following night, he tries another sleeping pill and enjoys a peaceful, undisturbed sleep. It would take a great deal of will-power to try to do without the pills under these circumstances, particularly if the patient does not know why he is getting the nightmares and that they will go away if only he has the patience to persist.

Another effect of barbiturates can start an even more dangerous cycle of drug dependency. Many people feel dizzy or headachy and sluggish when they wake up in the morning after a drug-induced sleep. Some have resorted to stimulants to get going again. Until a recent tightening of the drug regulations, drugs called amphetamines were commonly prescribed to give a mild "lift" to chronically tired or depressed patients. (Under such names as "bennies" or "speed," amphetamines are illegally taken by some people to produce a "high." But they can be extremely danger-ous, ruining physical health and producing mental aberrations.) The amphetamines keep the person so keyed up that he needs a sleeping pill to calm him down at night; then, with a barbiturate hangover in the morning, he needs another amphetamine to wake him up properly. Soon he is caught in an endless cycle. His body adapts to the drugs, and he soon finds that he needs increasing doses of both drugs to produce the same effect. If he is fortunate, a physician will help him to break the drug dependency before he has done irreparable harm to his body.

Oswald has discovered that amphetamines suppress REM sleep. Normally a person would not be able to fall asleep right after tak-ing an amphetamine, but when a barbiturate is taken along with it, sleep does result, and the REM-reducing effect is considerably greater than would be obtained with barbiturates alone.

Some sleeping drugs have been found to suppress not REM sleep, but stage 4 sleep instead. One of these is a new drug called Dalmane, which was tested recently in Anthony Kales' sleep labo-ratory. This drug, related to the tranquilizers Valium and Li-brium, was quite effective in putting patients to sleep, increasing total sleep time, and decreasing the number of awakenings during the night. Its manufacturers claim that it is extremely safe, producing no side effects except for a slight daytime drowsiness. Yet considering the results of studies of stage 4 sleep deprivation, what might be the long-term effects even of a "safe" drug such as Dalmane?

The search for safe and effective sleeping pills goes on. Many sleep researchers hope that answers will be found by imitating some of the body's own sleep chemicals, such as serotonin. Already, promising results have been obtained using the amino acid tryptophan and some chemically modified forms of it. This amino acid is commonly found in foods, and it is closely related to serotonin. Tryptophan has the curious ability to make some people fall very rapidly into REM sleep, rather than pass through the long sequence of stages 1 through 4 first. It can also produce an increase in the amount of time spent in deep sleep, and can cut down the number of awakenings during the night.

The effects of this amino acid on sleep first came to light quite accidentally. Sleep researcher Ian Oswald happened to be chatting with some friends from another department at the University of Edinburgh. These biologists were conducting a series of studies on rats involving tryptophan. Knowing of Oswald's interest in sleep, they casually mentioned an odd side effect they had discovered. Rats injected with tryptophan seemed to become sleepy, while other rats injected with salt water in a similar way did not. Oswald tried the amino acid on human volunteers, and a new piece of the puzzle of sleep chemistry fell into place.

In the search for safe and effective sleeping drugs, many other promising lines are being pursued. For example, the female sex hormone progesterone induces sleep quite effectively. This hormone is secreted in large amounts in the body of a pregnant woman, which is probably the explanation for the unusual sleepiness that women commonly feel during pregnancy. Researchers have a particular interest in following up this line of inquiry. Millions of women are now taking progesterone-like sex hormones in the form of birth-control pills, and these chemicals may be influencing their sleep patterns.

Meanwhile, a knowledge of how the standard sleep-inducing drugs change the quality of sleep has already suggested some possible applications. Drugs that suppress REM sleep, for example, may be used effectively by eye surgeons, who want to keep their patients' eyes from moving too much after eye surgery.

Evidence is accumulating that the mental excitement of REM sleep may actually be dangerous in certain medical conditions. For example, heart patients frequently awaken with severe chest pains, called angina. EEG studies have shown that these angina attacks are usually associated with REM periods. Questioning the sleepers about the dream they had just before they awoke has revealed that most of the dreams fall into two main categories: dreams involving vigorous physical activity, and dreams involving fear, anger, or frustration. Reducing REM sleep in heart patients might help to protect them from the agonizing pain of angina.

Ulcer patients, too, might benefit from REM-suppressers. Sleep researchers have discovered that people with duodenal ulcers secrete three to twenty times as much gastric juice at night as normal people. This juice is highly acid and can irritate the lining of the stomach and duodenum, causing the ulcer to get worse. The secretion of gastric juice rises sharply during REM periods in ulcer patients, although there is no such rise in people without ulcers.

Some sleep problems have been linked with stage 4 sleep, and might someday be treated with drugs that alter the pattern of deep sleep. The frightening experiences of night terrors, for example, occur in the depths of stage 4 sleep.

Another deep-sleep event, sleepwalking, is a curious phenomenon. Sleepwalkers have been known to walk about, drive cars, and engage in a variety of seemingly controlled activities, all while deeply asleep. One college student was discovered to have formed a habit of nightly outings. In the midst of stage 4 sleep, he would get dressed, walk three quarters of a mile from his dormitory to a nearby river, undress, take a swim, dress again, return to his dormitory room, change into his pajamas, and climb back into his bed. He had no awareness of what he was doing and did not recall the episodes in the morning.

To an observer, it seems that a sleepwalker is acting out a dream, yet if he is awakened, he may say that he does not recall anything. If a person with a tendency for sleepwalking is placed on his feet when he enters stage 4 sleep, he will begin to walk about, but a nonsleepwalker will not do so. Just before a somnambulistic (sleepwalking) episode, the EEG tracings usually show a burst of high-voltage, slow-wave activity. Such bursts may sometimes be observed in the EEG records of nonsleepwalkers, though much less frequently, and in them it never precedes sleepwalking.

Sleepwalking is rather common among children. Sleep researchers have noticed that the EEG patterns of these children seem to resemble those of normal children of younger ages. They theorize that somnambulistic episodes in children are connected with an immaturity in the nerve connections of the central nervous system. This condition tends to be outgrown in time; the sleepwalking child is not less intelligent or less well-adjusted than normal children.

Another deep-sleep problem for which researchers are searching for cures is bed-wetting. This occurs in as many as 15 percent of children (and in some adults as well); like sleepwalking, bedwetting is not usually associated with REM dreams, but instead takes place during non-REM sleep. Typically, a bed-wetting episode begins during stage 4 sleep, with the urine actually released as the child stirs and shifts to stage 2 or stage 1. If the subject is not awakened and changed after a bed-wetting episode, he does not descend into the deeper stages of sleep for several hours, and for the rest of the night, his REM periods may contain dreams of being wet.

Some physicians believe that bed-wetting is frequently linked to emotional problems. Others attribute it to an immaturity of systems of the body; like sleepwalking, the condition usually disappears with the passage of time.

Drugs are one approach to the problems of troubled sleep. The Russians have come up with another approach: the use of electricity. It had been known for some time that electrodes implanted in certain regions of the brain could be used to stimulate sleep centers and put an animal to sleep. About two decades ago, it was discovered in the Soviet Union that extremely minute currents of electricity, applied to the brain through electrodes that could be worn in the form of a pair of eyepads, could put some people to sleep. Researchers named this sleep machine *elektroson*, which in Russian literally means "electric sleep."

A person receiving an electric sleep treatment does not feel the tiny current that is applied. There may be a slight tingling at first, while the current is being adjusted (the exact current and placement of the electrodes must be determined for each individual), but then nothing. Electric-shock therapy, used in treating some severe mental disorders, produces violent convulsions and leaves the patient in a state of mental confusion that may persist for months. But the mild currents of electric sleep treatments do not seem to have any negative aftereffects. Indeed, in most cases, the subject feels pleasantly refreshed.

Although electric sleep therapy has been used regularly in the Soviet Union for decades, and extensive investigations are now under way in Austria, Germany, Israel, and various other countries, United States sleep researchers, for the most part, have been highly skeptical. One reason for their skepticism was that early studies of imported elektrosons quickly revealed that they put only about half the subjects to sleep. Yet even those who were not put to sleep generally reported a feeling of pleasant relaxation, and they were often as refreshed as though they had actually slept.

Another reason for American skepticism lay in the astonishing claims that have been made for electric sleep therapy. It has been said to be successful in the treatment of such varied conditions as recurrent headaches, asthma, eczema, gastritis, hypertension, ulcers, toxemia of pregnancy, anxiety, depression, insomnia. . . . Any treatment purported to take care of that great a variety of ills literally sounds too good to be true.

Yet some corroborated reports of carefully controlled studies have come in. In a study at Massachusetts General Hospital in Boston, two-thirds of a group of fifty patients showed pronounced emotional changes after electrosleep treatments. If the current at the forehead electrode was positive, most of the patients became moody and depressed; when the electrode was negative, there was a remarkable rise in spirits, even among patients who had been suffering from severe depression.

Numerous studies on much larger numbers of patients, both in the Soviet Union and elsewhere, have revealed equally striking results. Many of these experiments included safeguards to eliminate the possibility that suggestion, rather than the electricity, might be producing the effects. In one Russian study of 2,500 patients, only 1,000 actually received the treatment. For the other 1,500 patients, the doctors only pretended to turn the current on. Definite improvement was noted among the patients who received the electrosleep treatment, while no change was observed in the others.

The effects of electric sleep treatments on normal sleeping patterns seem to vary with the individual. For some people, the nightly sleep periods were lengthened. Others found themselves able to get along with only a few hours of sleep a night as long as they continued the treatments during the day. Long-term studies on animals seem to indicate that the treatments are safe. Perhaps the time is not far off when a person with sleep problems will be able to go to a sleep clinic equipped with an "electric dormitory."

NINE
How To Get a Good Night's Sleep

Do you have a special routine for getting to sleep? Perhaps you always drink a glass of warm milk before you go to bed. Just before you turn out the light, you may read a few pages from a book or whisper a special prayer. Perhaps you do not turn out all the lights, but prefer to leave one burning. Are you one of the people who cannot sleep unless a window is open, even on the coldest nights? Or would you rather have your bedroom snug and warm? Do you usually sleep with someone else, or do you sleep alone? Do you have some special object that you always take to bed with you? (If you do, don't be ashamed to admit it, thinking it is a childish habit you should have outgrown. A number of famous people sleep with a teddy bear or a special pillow or some other favorite object.)

Man's whole written history and the oral traditions of folklore abound with prescriptions for getting a good night's sleep. Modern sleep research is providing a wealth of information that can be used to assess the value of these age-old suggestions.

"Early to bed, early to rise," for example, may be good advice for the "larks," whose daily temperature cycles rise quickly to a midmorning peak. But it could mean a lifetime of torture for a confirmed "owl," who wakes up grouchy, starts slowly, does not reach a temperature peak until afternoon or evening, and is still raring to go at midnight.

Even the amount of sleep we need seems uncertain. Studies have shown that some people do quite nicely on a regular six or seven hours of sleep a night, while others need nine hours or even more. Some supersleepers have even been studied. These people normally sleep only three or four hours a night, but their EEG records show that they are able to get much more deep sleep and REM sleep into their short sleeping periods than would normally be expected. Somehow they have acquired the ability to sleep more efficiently than most people do, shuttling back and forth between deep sleep and REM sleep and "wasting" very little time on the lighter intermediate stages.

Many of the good sleep prescriptions that have been handed down through the ages boil down to a simple formula: keep regular habits and stay healthy. This seems to make good sense, and modern sleep experiments have verified that individual aspects of the formula are quite valid.

Regular habits, for example, fit neatly into the concept of circadian rhythms. Your body systems all have their own rhythms, which ebb and flow like a tide with each twenty-four-hour period. If you go to bed at about the same time each night and get up at about the same time each morning, your body rhythms can adapt readily to the pattern. But if you try to go to bed at an odd hour when you are not normally sleepy, or try to stay up long past the time when your body cycles begin to ebb, then why be surprised if your sleep patterns are at least temporarily upset?

What about exercise? Certainly a regular program of moderate exercise is a good thing for your general health and well-being, and for this reason it should help your sleep as well. But have you

The great American inventor Thomas Edison said that he didn't get more than five hours' sleep each night. But he did nap in his lab during long workdays. Even on an outing with President Warren Harding and industrialist Harvey Firestone, he managed to get forty winks.

ever-felt too tired to sleep after a strenuous day of unusually heavy exercise? Studies at Downstate Medical Center in Brooklyn and in other sleep laboratories indicate that regular moderate exercise can help both sleep and general health, in particular, producing larger amounts of refreshing, deep sleep. Exercising in the afternoon seemed to have a better effect than exercising shortly before bedtime, but even that was better than no exercise at all. However, unusually heavy exercise can produce a night of fitful, unsatisfying sleep.

What about the traditional glass of warm milk? Milk is very high in proteins, which are made up of amino acids. One of the amino acids, tryptophan, has been found to produce sleep, possibly by being transformed in the body into the sleep chemical serotonin. Milk might be regarded as a natural mild sedative.

The old wives' tale about not eating a full meal too close to bedtime may have some truth to it, too. During sleep, the secretions of digestive juices are normally reduced. If the stomach must cope with a full load of food, it may keep other systems of the body stimulated and, through the reticular activating system in the brain, keep the whole body in a state of wakefulness.

Worries can keep your RAS in a state of excitement, too. People who suffer from insomnia often lie awake for hours, brooding about unhappy experiences or unsolved problems. Curiously, one of the most frequent worries of insomniacs is about losing sleep. The more they worry about not being able to fall asleep, the wider awake they become.

What if you are lying in bed trying to go to sleep, and you suddenly notice the ticking of the clock? (Even electric clocks make noises, and they sound much louder during the night than they do in the daytime because the brain is not receiving as many other stimuli from the sense organs to compete with them.) What if there is an annoying noise outside that won't stop? What if you are sleeping with someone who keeps snoring or pulling the covers off you?

Try to relax. A human being is capable of sleeping through an amazing variety of unpleasant circumstances without apparently minding them at all. Imagine a volunteer sleeping in a laboratory, wired to an EEG machine. One sleep researcher says that wearing a blood-pressure cuff on your ankle feels like having a shark grabbing you by the leg and pulling you under—and yet people fall asleep quite successfully wearing blood-pressure cuffs.

In one series of experiments on a group of Oxford University students, sleep researchers wanted to determine whether the volunteers could distinguish their own names and the names of other people while they were asleep, and also whether the names would

Trying to get settled for a good sleep in the lab looks more difficult than it actually turns out to be.

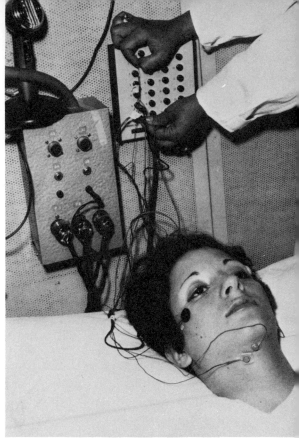

be incorporated into their dreams. But there was always the possibility that just the stimulus of hearing a voice speaking would rouse the subjects, and not the specific names at all. So the researchers trained their subjects to sleep through an endless tape recording of nonsense syllables.

If sleep volunteers sleep through a whole night of recorded nonsense syllables, are you going to let a little thing like an electric clock bother you? Relax, and give your body a chance to adjust.

TEN
The Long Sleeps

Have you ever awakened on a frosty winter morning, with a chill penetrating the air and bleak grayness outside your window, and wished you could just turn over and sleep until spring? Sleep is often used as a means of escape from unpleasant situations, but even the most maladjusted humans do not usually resort to such extreme measures to avoid the rigors of winter. Many members of the animal kingdom, however, do precisely this. By entering long periods of sleep or torpidity, lasting for weeks or even months at a time, they are able to survive the cold and scarcity of food that winter brings.

To a great degree, the cold-blooded animals, or poikilotherms, are at the mercy of their environment. Some heat is produced, of course, by the action of their muscles and by the burning of body fats. But reptiles, amphibians, fishes, and invertebrates cannot control their own body temperature, and they are generally just a few degrees warmer than the air or water surrounding them. A cold-blooded fish swimming in tropical waters near the equator may have a body that is quite warm—just as warm as that of most warm-blooded birds or mammals. But place the same fish in an icebox, and its temperature will begin to fall, until it reaches approximately the temperature of its environment.

Chemists have found, as a general rule of thumb, that the speed of chemical reactions tends to double each time the temperature is raised about 10°C (or about 18°F). The chemical reactions of the body are no exception. When an animal's body is cooled, the thousands of chemical reactions that go on in its blood and organs slow down, almost to a standstill if the temperature is lowered sufficiently. This drop in the rate of body reactions with falling temperature has both advantages and disadvantages. These reactions consume energy, which an animal must continually replace by eating. But during the winter, food is scarce. The leaves and fruits have fallen from the trees, and grasses and other low-growing plants are either dead or withered or covered with a layer of snow. Many insects have died, leaving only winter eggs to provide a new generation for their species in the spring. Others are hidden away under stones or in crevices in the bark of trees. Other small prey animals, too, do not run about as freely as they do in the warm seasons of the year. The lowered winter temperatures of a poikilotherm help it to conserve energy. With its body reactions damped down, it does not move, barely breathes, and its heart scarcely beats at all. Its energy needs are so small that it does not have to feed; it can survive this dormant time using up the reserves of starch and fats stored in its own body.

Winter torpor helps cold-blooded animals to get through the cold season of the year, but it is an adaptation that carries some dangers. A hibernating reptile, amphibian, or insect cannot rouse itself. It can be roused when the temperature of its environment rises, but it cannot generate the heat needed to warm its own body to cope with an emergency situation. One of the most dangerous emergencies a hibernating animal may face is freezing. Ice crystals form in the blood and tissues, bursting and tearing the delicate cells. If too many cells are destroyed, the animal dies. A poikilo-therm cannot produce heat to keep its body temperature safely above the freezing point when the outside temperature falls.

Animals that hibernate, spending the winter in a torpid state, usually prepare for the cold season by finding or digging them-selves a safe refuge, beyond the reach of the frost. Toads and snakes hibernate in burrows in the soil, down beneath the frost line. (It is no coincidence that few animals hibernate in the per-mafrost regions of the world, where a layer of soil is permanently frozen hard.)

Garden snails, too, hibernate in burrows. The snail digs its burrow in the soil under a log or leaf litter, using its muscular foot to make the hole. Snug in the bottom of the burrow, it turns itself with the opening of its shell upward and covers the opening with a membrane. A tiny breathing hole remains in the otherwise tight seal, but the snail barely breathes in comparison with its ac-tive state. Its respiration rate drops from fifty to sixty movements per minute down to a mere four to twelve per minute during hi-bernation. When the snail emerges from its burrow in the spring, it has lost weight—it has been living on its stored body fats.

In the autumn, frogs bury themselves in the mud at the bot-toms of ponds. They are unmoving through the winter, and their body processes are nearly stilled. Although they breathe air through their lungs when they are active, frogs can survive the tor-pid season surrounded by water and mud. An exchange of gases through their skin brings in a little oxygen from the water, and this is enough for their greatly reduced needs. In shallow ponds, particularly man-made ponds with a concrete bottom, frogs and fishes will die in the winter, when all the water freezes.

A great variety of cold-blooded animals pass the cold winter in a state of torpor, from turtles to toads, from bumblebee queens to mosquitoes. The slowdown of their body processes caused by the low temperature permits them to conserve energy and survive without feeding, using up their stored body fats.

But what of the warm-blooded animals, or homeotherms? In their natural habitats, they have the ability to keep their bodies at a relatively constant temperature, no matter what the temperature may be outside. The body of a homeotherm is something like a house equipped with efficient heating and air-conditioning systems, both controlled by an automatic thermostat that switches on either the heating or the cooling system as needed to keep the temperature of the house comfortable.

Warm-bloodedness has important advantages: although chemical reactions speed up with rising temperatures, too much heat can damage the delicate organic molecules of life. There is thus an optimum temperature, a compromise providing enough heat for the body reactions to proceed at a good rate, yet not enough to harm the enzymes and other chemicals needed for these reactions. Homeotherms can keep their body temperatures just at this optimum value and remain alert and active no matter what the season of the year.

But this delicate temperature control is an expensive process, in terms of energy. Homeotherms must eat continually to refuel their energy reserves. Yet in the winter, warm-blooded animals, too, find it difficult to get enough to eat. Indeed, if they remain active, they need even more food than usual because they must expend great quantities of energy to heat their bodies high above the temperature of the environment. If the outside temperature falls too low, their heat-producing capacity may not be able to keep pace. Then the body temperature gradually falls, and the animals may ultimately die.

Some homeotherms solve the problem by avoiding the cold entirely. They migrate in the fall to regions closer to the equator, which will remain warm when winter comes to their summer homes. Others busy themselves in the late summer and fall, storing up caches of food to last them over the lean times to come. A squirrel, hiding acorns in a hollow tree, has chosen that answer to the problem of winter. But many animals have the ability to temporarily turn down their body thermostats, just as a thrifty homeowner turns down the thermostat of his house at night to save fuel. These warm-blooded animals may sleep through much of the cold season or may even enter a torpor just as profound as that of the true poikilotherms.

The animal whose name most frequently comes to mind when the subject of hibernation is mentioned is the bear. As winter approaches, the bear eats ravenously, putting on a thick layer of fat. When it is fat enough, it stops eating. Alaskan guides on Kodiak Island say that the bears there gorge themselves on wild cranberries just before they are ready to retire for their winter sleep. These wild berries act as a purge, leaving the bear's intestines as clean as though they had been washed with soap and water. A bear may top off its autumn gorging with a meal of fibrous roots or pine needles. These remain in the end of its intestines as a firm plug, called a tappen. The bear's stomach contracts into a hard knot, and it will neither eat nor defecate again until spring.

Now the bear takes refuge in a den, in a cave or in the shelter of a tangled thicket. It will sleep for days or weeks at a time, or even the whole winter through. The fattest bears are the most likely to continue sleeping. It is the lean bears, those that were not able to prepare well enough for winter, which may awaken and prowl irritably about the forest for a few hours or days before returning to their slumbers. As the weeks pass, the bear's fat reserves are gradually exhausted. When it emerges from its den in the spring, it is gaunt and hungry.

Considering the bear's fame as a hibernator, it may seem surprising that scientists generally do not classify it as a true hibernator at all. There are a number of reasons for this. A bear's winter sleep is fitful. It is easily roused, and it can return to its normal, active self within a few minutes. During its winter sleep, the bear breathes relatively normally, and its body temperature is only a little below its usual level—perhaps 81°F or so.

Raccoons, skunks, and chipmunks are some other warm-

As the waterfowl fly south for the winter, the fattened bears look to their caves for a long winter of inactivity.

blooded mammals that are classified as winter sleepers, rather than true hibernators. The chipmunk, for example, lays in a store of grains or nuts during the fall, tucking them away in a neat pile in the bottom of its burrow. A soft layer of grass completes the winter bed, and it retires to nap the cold time away. Whenever it is hungry, the chipmunk wakes, nibbles a meal from the storehouse under its mattress, and goes back to sleep.

The behavior of a true hibernator is quite different. The woodchuck, for example, can be seen in the summer and early fall in fields and meadows, busily stuffing itself with food. From May to

September it doubles its weight. By the time it is ready to retire for the winter, it can barely squeeze in and out of its burrow.

At last the fat woodchuck curls itself into a tight ball inside its cramped burrow and begins to enter the state of hibernation. It is not a smooth and steady transition. First the animal's heartbeat and respiration rate begin to fall, and then its body temperature drops. From time to time the woodchuck shivers convulsively, and its body temperature rises briefly, only to fall again to a new, lower level. After about a week, it seems to be a true poikilotherm: its body temperature is only a degree or two above the temperature of its environment. Other changes are equally dramatic. From a normal heartbeat of about eighty per minute, it has dropped to a mere three or four. It seems incredible that such sluggish circulation could provide enough nourishment to keep the woodchuck's brain and other vital organs alive; it is aided by the fact that the blood vessels in its limbs and most parts of its body are greatly narrowed. If you cut its toe, it would scarcely bleed. Its breathing, too, has dropped almost to the vanishing point. An active woodchuck breathes about twenty-five times a minute; in hibernation, a breath can be observed only every five minutes or so. It hardly seems alive, and it will remain in this state for five or six months. When it emerges in the spring, it will have lost a third of its weight or more.

A deep hibernator like the woodchuck seems to have been transformed into a poikilotherm. But the 'chuck retains one important advantage that cold-blooded animals do not possess: it is not completely at the mercy of its environment. Its body temperature follows the temperature of the environment only down to a certain level. As the freezing point is approached, the woodchuck's body remains about ten degrees Fahrenheit above freezing. If the outside temperature falls so far that this temperature cannot be maintained, an automatic alarm mechanism is set off: the woodchuck wakes up.

Arousal from hibernation is a complex process. First heat is generated in a special layer of dark-brown fat between the shoulder blades. This brown fat is an amazingly efficient heat producer, which warms the animal like an electric blanket. Its cells are much larger than the cells in the normal white fat, and they release heat twenty times as fast. The front part of the woodchuck's body warms quickly under its "electric blanket," and its heart begins to beat faster. Respiration speeds up, soon returning to normal. Its eyelids twitch, and its forepaws move feebly. The heart beats strongly now, even faster than normal, and the blood vessels through the body dilate. The strengthened flow of blood nourishes the body muscles, and the woodchuck begins to shiver violently. This violent muscle action generates still more heat, and within a few hours the animal is back to its normal state.

Arousing from hibernation consumes an enormous amount of energy. Researchers have computed that one arousal uses up as much of an animal's fat reserves as ten days of hibernation. Obviously, a hibernator cannot afford to rouse too often, if it is to survive the winter.

Curiously, there is one important errand that does wake the woodchuck in the midst of its winter sleep. It generally awakens around February, while snow is still on the ground and food is not yet available. It is driven out of its burrow by the urge to mate. Diving through the snow, the male locates the burrow of a female woodchuck and starts a new generation on its way. This function attended to, it retires to its burrow again. (In this the woodchuck is unusual; most other animals remain active once they have left their hibernating den.)

Observations of other typical deep hibernators, including the marmot (a European woodchuck), the hedgehog (a European insectivore that relies on a coat of sharp spines for protection from its enemies), the dormouse (a bushy-tailed European rodent whose name comes from the French word "to sleep"), the hamster, and the ground squirrel have revealed patterns very similar to the woodchuck's. The heartbeat, which may be several hundred per minute in the active state (500 for the hamster), is slowed to just a few beats per minute. The respiration rate is lowered to just a few per minute or even less. In fact, the hibernator's need for oxygen is so reduced that it can even survive surprisingly long exposures to an atmosphere without any oxygen at all. Hibernating hedgehogs survived exposures to an atmosphere without oxygen for up to two hours without any ill effects, whereas in the normal state they could stand only a few minutes without air. One English researcher kept a hibernating marmot in pure carbon dioxide for four hours, and it recovered satisfactorily. Hibernators seem so far removed from awareness of the external world that they do not awake even if they are plunged into a bucket of water, rolled across the table like a ball, or stuck with pins.

Researchers do not seem to be in agreement on the electrical activity of the brains of hibernators. All report a great reduction of the amplitude of the EEG signals (the height of the waves on a graph of the electrical activity of the brain). But reports differ on whether the EEG recordings show the normal type of activity, merely reduced to about 10 percent of the normal amplitude, or an actual "EEG silence"—no electrical signals at all. Experiments with electrodes implanted in the brain have shown that the electrical activity in different parts of the brain is restored to normal at different temperature levels, and these temperatures also vary with the species.

All these precise studies have been possible because hibernators generally hibernate just as readily in the laboratory as in their natural environment. Indeed, some animals will go into hibernation at the appropriate time of year even under conditions that would seem to make hibernation unnecessary. The golden-mantled ground squirrel, for example, was found to hibernate from October to May, even if it was kept in a warm room with twelve hours of artificial daylight and given all the food and water it could use. Yet in other species, the entrance into hibernation seems to be triggered by falling temperatures, or a lack of food, or the length of the day or night.

The whole problem of how the complex mechanisms of hibernation are triggered is receiving a great deal of study and has yielded much interesting information, though few definitive answers as yet.

Glands of the endocrine system definitely seem to be involved. The pituitary—the master gland that regulates the functions of the other endocrine glands—has been observed to shrink during hibernation and swell as the time for arousal approaches. Some researchers have caused woodchucks and hedgehogs to enter hibernation by injections of insulin, the hormone of the pancreas. Insulin works to reduce the amount of sugar (glucose) in the blood, and as might be expected, injections of glucose caused a hibernating woodchuck to arouse. Other experiments seem to indicate involvement of the adrenal gland and the thyroid gland, but the results of different researchers are contradictory.

The rabbit is a small field animal that, unlike many of its neighbors, does not hibernate during the winter, but does sleep off and on.

ROGER KERKHAM

When deposits of brown fat were discovered in the bodies of hibernators, it was quickly concluded that this must be the mysterious "hibernation gland" that controls the whole process. An experiment by the German researcher C. F. Wendt seems to supply some corroboration. He injected material from the brown fat of a hibernating hedgehog into rats. The rats, which are not normally hibernators, quickly became listless, and the rate of their body reactions dropped sharply. Injections of olive oil did not produce such effects. But later researchers tend to deny that the brown fat is really an endocrine gland and believe that it simply acts as a highly efficient heat generator.

Some recent experiments indicate that the sleep chemical serotonin works in the lowering of the body temperature and maintaining hibernation. In one experiment conducted by Soviet researchers, for example, an amino acid, 5-hydroxytryptophan, which is converted to serotonin in the body, was injected into hibernating susliks (a kind of ground squirrel). The injections slowed down the process of arousal and the rise in body temperature that normally accompanies it.

Nearly all the warm-blooded hibernators that have been observed belong to the groups of rodents or insect-eaters. But from ancient times, there have been stories of hibernating birds. Closer observations usually revealed that mistakes had been made, and the birds that mysteriously disappeared in the winter were usually found to be migrating, not hibernating. The whole subject fell into such disrepute that for a long time scientists were afraid even to mention the possibility seriously, for fear of embarrassing themselves among their colleagues.

The topic of hibernation among birds was finally reestablished as a respectable subject for scientific investigation in 1946. Edmund C. Jaeger, a professor at Riverside College in California, happened by sheer chance on a poorwill, nestled in a small depression in the granite rocks of the Chuckawalla Mountains of the Colorado desert. The little bird seemed to be dead. No heartbeat or breathing movements could be detected; no moisture formed on a cold mirror placed in front of its nostrils, and there was no response when a strong beam of light was focused on the pupils of its eyes. Yet when Professor Jaeger replaced the bird in its crevice, it lazily opened one eye and shut it again. Two days later, the investigator returned and found the bird still in the same place, in exactly the same position. He placed a numbered ring on the poorwill's leg and continued to observe it from time to time. Through the winter, the bird's temperature was about 64° F, or about forty degrees below normal, and its body weight continued to decline, until it had lost about a third of its active weight. The same bird was found in the same rock crevice for four winters in a row.

Few hibernating poorwills have been found in the wild, but these birds can be made to hibernate in the laboratory by lowering the air temperature to 38° F. Interestingly, although scientists long disdained to consider seriously the possibility of birds' hibernating, the Hopi Indians were apparently aware of the poorwill's habits. Their name for the bird is *Holchko,* The Sleeping One. Now that the subject has again become respectable in scientific circles, researchers are following up other early reports of hibernation among such birds as the North American whippoorwill (a relative of the poorwill), the Australian frogmouth, and various swifts, hummingbirds, and swallows.

A great variety of animals thus use sleep or hibernation as a means of surviving the cold and food scarcity of winter. A number of other animals (and sometimes the same ones) use similar mechanisms to get through another period of hardship in the natural world, the hot, dry spells of midsummer. The term hibernation comes from the Latin word *hibernus,* meaning wintry. The term for summer torpor, estivation, is similarly formed from a Latin word for summer, *aestas.*

Studies seem to indicate that estivation is triggered by a lack of food, although a lack of water may make the animal stop eating.

Although the triggering mechanisms are different, the processes of hibernation and estivation are very similar. The animal is in a state of deep torpor; curled into a tight ball, it does not eat, its body temperature is lower than normal, and the rate of its life processes is greatly reduced. Many chemical reactions in the body, particularly those of digestion, produce heat as a by-product. Estivation thus not only provides a way to get along when food is scarce, but helps in the body's struggle to maintain a comfortable temperature during the hottest times of the year.

The ground squirrel is a deep estivator. When the summer grasses turn brown under the hot sun, and ponds and streams are drying up, this little rodent is curled into a ball in a grass-lined, underground sleeping chamber. Its body is cold, and so rigid that it cannot be readily uncurled. It seems lifeless, and pinching or shaking will not rouse it. Indeed, it looks precisely as it does when it hibernates in the winter.

Chipmunks also disappear during the hot, dry periods of mid-summer. But the chipmunk is only a partial sleeper, not a true estivator. Snug in its leaf-lined burrow in the cool earth, it sleeps and conserves energy. Its body temperature is lower than normal, but it rouses easily if it is disturbed.

Many cold-blooded animals estivate. Snails, frogs, toads, and a number of fish can wait out a dry spell in the mud at the bottom of a dried-out pond and come to life again when the autumn rains fill the pond with water. The lungfishes of Africa, Australia, and South America dig a burrow in the bottom mud as their pools begin to dry up. These fish have primitive lungs and can breathe in oxygen from the air. The tunnel leading to a lungfish's burrow provides a lifeline of air. Coiled tightly with a cocoon-like case enclosing its body, it waits in a dormant state for the flooding rains.

Perhaps the champion estivators are tropical snails, which can remain dormant for months or even years at a time without ill effects. In one recorded instance, in 1846 the British Museum received the shell of an Egyptian land snail, which was assumed to be empty. The specimen was fastened to an identification card, properly labeled, and filed away. Then, in 1850, traces of slime were noticed on the card. It was placed in water, and the snail promptly poked its head and foot out and began to crawl.

These long periods of winter or summer dormancy have many parallels to sleep. Indeed, for bears, skunks, chipmunks, and others that are not considered true hibernators, extended periods of sleep are used to escape the rigors of extreme cold or heat and lack of food. But is true hibernation—the strange ability of homeotherms to temporarily give up their temperature regulation and become apparent poikilotherms—a form of sleep? Although some researchers have claimed to see connections between hibernation and sleep, the tendency today is to regard them as two equally fascinating but quite separate phenomena.

ELEVEN
The Future of Sleep Research

Bedtime sometimes seems to arrive at the most inconvenient point of the day. There is a book we'd love to finish, a fascinating "late late show" listed in the television guide, a party that is still going strong—but we reluctantly realize that if we indulge the whim and cut our sleep short, we will suffer for it the next day.

It is therefore not surprising that although much of the sleep research is directed toward understanding the mechanisms of normal sleep and helping people who have trouble sleeping to find rest, considerable efforts are also being directed toward making sleep more efficient, so that its total length can be reduced, or at least to finding ways to harness some of this "wasted" time to some useful purpose.

One of these areas, which has received much publicity but so far has shown little progress, is sleep learning. There are kits on the market that promise to perform miracles of rapid learning by playing recordings of the subject to you while you sleep. Foreign languages, self-confidence—a fantastic gamut of subjects is of-

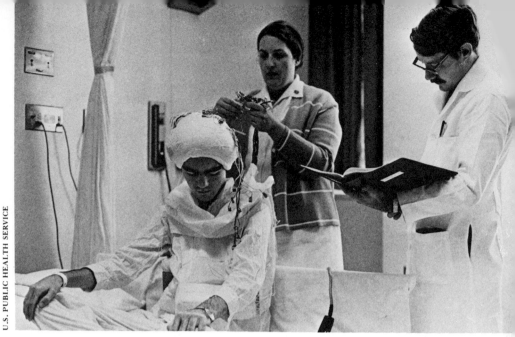

Learning does indeed take place during periods of sleep. The only questions are how much, how effectively, and during what periods. Researchers are working on the answers to these problems.

fered. Meanwhile, in the Soviet Union, dormitory facilities are being set up for teaching people dull but necessary information such as foreign language vocabularies.

Does sleep learning really work? The few controlled scientific investigations have been mainly discouraging. In an experiment in a London hospital, volunteers were divided into three groups in an effort to determine whether people can learn pairs of nonsense syllables while asleep. All of the volunteers had shown themselves to be quite good at such learning exercises when they were awake. Now, during the night, a pillow speaker played fifteen pairs of nonsense syllables into the ears of the first group. The second group heard the same syllables, but scrambled into different orders. The third group was treated to recorded music. In each case, the recorder played only when EEG tracings showed that the sleeper was in a period of deep sleep.

In the morning, all the subjects were tested to see how quickly they could learn the correct group of nonsense syllables. If learning could take place during deep sleep, the researchers expected that the first group would be able to master the list of syllables more rapidly than the members of the third group. The second group should take longer, on the average, because they would have been confused by the scrambled list.

When the results were in, there was no significant difference in the learning rates of the three groups. The researchers interpreted this result as an indication that no sleep learning had taken place.

In a way, this experiment was not entirely fair. Most of the sleep-learning techniques now being used claim to have their effect during the period of drowsiness just before sleep and the light stages of sleep itself. You may have used a somewhat similar learning technique yourself. If you are trying to learn a poem, for example, and you repeat it to yourself just before you go to bed, you may find it firmly fixed in your mind when you wake up. Scientists believe that this technique works because the brain has an opportunity to work efficiently on the last thing you think of before you go to sleep because no other stimuli follow to distract it.

Indeed, you may find when you wake up that you have an answer to a problem that was bothering you before you went to bed. This effect has been observed in sleep laboratories. In one study the subjects were presented with a problem just before bedtime: "The letters O, T, T, F, F, S, S form the beginning of a well-known series. Once you have broken the code, you will be able to add an infinite number of letters to the series." Most of the subjects were unable to figure out the answer while they were awake, but many of them had the answer by the next morning. Some even reported the answer in the dreams they related when they were awakened during REM periods. (The answer is: "*One, Two, Three, Four, Five, Six, Seven.*")

Studies have indicated that some learning can take place during drowsiness and even light sleep, but in general the mind is not sharp during these periods, and any learning that does occur is rather inefficient. In addition, it has not yet been determined whether the sleep-learner may pay a price for his lessons. The disturbance that the tape recording produces in the normal pattern of sleep may cause a person to sleep less restfully or to sleep longer in order to get his normal quota.

Much more promise seems to lie in experiments indicating that people can learn to control the quality of their sleep itself. At the Langley Porter Neuropsychiatric Institute in San Francisco, Joe Kamiya has trained people to recognize their own alpha rhythms and produce them at will. He used a technique called "alpha feedback" to accomplish this. A volunteer would lie quietly in the laboratory bedroom while his brain waves were recorded by an EEG machine. A bell would ring from time to time, and each time the volunteer would be asked to guess whether or not his brain was sending out the alpha rhythm. He was immediately informed whether he was correct or not, and in a short time the bell would ring again. Soon the volunteers were able to guess correctly all the time. Then they were able to tell the experimenter whenever they felt the alpha rhythm appear. Now the EEG hookup was adjusted so that whenever the subject showed an alpha rhythm, a buzzer rang. The subject was instructed either to try to keep the bell ringing or to turn it off. The volunteers mastered this feat with ease, and some even developed the ability to speed up or slow down their alpha rhythms when asked to do so.

People who have learned to identify their alpha rhythms describe the alpha state as a state of pleasant relaxation. There have been some indications—though no controlled scientific studies as yet—that periods of alpha relaxation may even be able to substitute for part of a normal night's sleep.

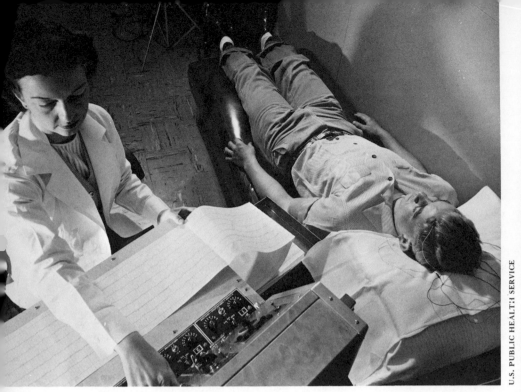

Volunteers can be educated to recognize different kinds of sleep, and even to signal researchers when they are having dreams.

Meanwhile, there is some evidence that people can learn to recognize and control not only a waking alpha rhythm, but even specific states of sleep as well. At Yale University, Neal Miller trained cats to enter a state of mind that produced spindle patterns on their EEGs. Normally, these spindles occur only in stage 2 and stage 3 sleep. It was hard to tell if the cat was actually sleeping while it was producing the spindle patterns; it stood rigidly and stared off into space. Miller used a system of rewards to train the cat. An electrode was implanted in the pleasure center of its hypothalamus. Whenever the cat showed spindles in its EEG, the implanted electrode was stimulated. Soon the animal was producing the spindles with great frequency to get its electrical reward. Then the researcher changed the rules, and began to reward an arousal pattern instead. The cat quickly adjusted and changed its response to produce an arousal EEG.

In another experiment, Judith and John Antrobus, working with Charles Fisher in New York City, trained three nurses to distinguish the REM stage of sleep. Each volunteer slept with a microswitch taped to her forefinger, and was instructed to give one signal for dreaming and another for sleep without dreams. The women had difficulty in learning to signal from nondreaming sleep, but they became quite adept at signaling from REM sleep periods. (One woman dreamed all night that she was an Indian sending smoke signals.) Then the Antrobuses tried waking the volunteers at various points in their sleep and asking them to guess whether they were in "A" sleep (REM sleep) or "B" sleep (stage 2 sleep). Each time the women were told immediately whether they were right or not and then allowed to fall back asleep. One nurse not only learned to distinguish the two types of sleep, but could tell when she was in a different stage as well. In other laboratories, volunteers have been trained to awaken spontaneously at the end of REM periods and record their dreams.

Will we some day be able to tune in on the rich fantasy life of our nighttime minds and control both the quality and the quantity of our own sleep at will? This is an exciting frontier of modern sleep research.

Index

acetone, 59
acetylcholine, 100-101, 104
addiction to sleeping pills, 118, 123
adrenalin, 101-102, 116
adults: periods in REM sleep of, 87;
    sleep patterns of, 14, 32
Alcmeon, ancient theory on sleep, 96
Allison, Truett, 39, 46, 48, 49, 50, 52
"alpha feedback," 151
alpha relaxation, 151
alpha rhythms, 60-61, 151-152
amphetamines, cycle of sleeping pills
    and, 123
amphibians: cold-blooded, 134; hi-
    bernation of, 135
anger center, 96
antihistamines, 32, 118
Antrobus, Judith and John, 153
ants, sleeping behavior of, 34-35
Aserinsky, Eugene, 76-79
astronauts, 17-18, 22, 29, 32

baboon, 40
barbiturates, 118, 122, 123
bat: habits of, 52; lifespan of, in com-
    parison to shrew, 52
beans, "sleep movements" of, 20, 25
bear, hibernation of, 138, 147
bed-wetting, 84, 126-127
bees: biological clocks of, 26-27; navi-
    gating abilities of, 26
Berger, Hans, 56
biotelemetry devices, 32
birds: hibernation of, 144-145; sleep-
    ing positions of, 47; variations in
    sleep habits of, 46-47
birth-control pills, 124-125
blind people, dream experiences of,
    86-87
body temperature cycles, daily, 21,
    130
Bokert, Edward, 90
brain: alertness of, during sleep, 14;

function and description of, 55-56; in sleep learning, 150; parts of, 96-98

brain waves, 16-17, 83. *See also* EEG

brainstem, 96; damage of, 98; injection of acetylcholine into, 100-101; injection of adrenalin into, 101; nuclei of raphe of, 101; "wake up" centers in, 99

breathing center, 96

Brown, Frank A., Jr., 27-28

butterflies, sleeping position of, 34

Caton, Richard, 56

cats: as predators, 39; deprivation of REM sleep in, 114-115; dreaming of, 44-45; EEG tracings of, while asleep, 40-42; effect of acetylcholine on, 100-101; experiments on, 104, 152-153; kittens, newborn, 44; sleeping habits of, in laboratory, 39

cavies, 40

cerebellum, 96-97

cerebral cortex: alert, 99-100; electrodes in, 40; functions of, 98; nerve connections of, 99

cerebrum, 98

chimpanzees, sleep habits of, in laboratory, 38-39

chipmunk: as a partial sleeper, 146; as a winter sleeper, 139, 147

chloral hydrate, 122

circadian rhythm, 130; change in, 22; in animals, 21, 25; in plants, 20, 25

control centers of brain, 96, 98

coordination of muscle activities, 97

cycle of sleep and wakefulness, 16

Dalmane, 123-124

day lily flowers, 20

Dement, William, 77-79, 85-86, 90, 114-115

diurnal creatures, 21

dog: appearance of, while sleeping, 33; as predator, 39

dormouse, hibernation of, 141

"dream books," 72-73

dreams: color of, 79, 92-93; incorporation of real experiences into, 88-90; interpretation of, in ancient times, 70-72, 93; main functions of, 74-75; material for, 88-94; number of, each night, 69; predictive role of, 70, 72-73; relation of eating certain foods to, 79-80; remembering of, 80-82; self-image in, 70; Sigmund Freud's interpretations of, 73-75, 89; subjects of, 69

drowsy state, 61

ducks, sleeping habits of, 47-48

echidnas, sleep research on, 49-50

Edison, Thomas Alva, 14, 16

electric-shock therapy, 127

electrochemical reactions, 55-56

EEG (electroencephalogram), 16, 37, 40, 42, 46, 50, 77, 86, 99, 132; derivation of term, 54-55; during hibernation, 142; in controlling quality of sleep, 151; in determining effects of sleeping pills, 120; in insomnia, 116; in scoring active or passive dreams, 85; in short sleep periods, 130; in sleep learning, 150; in sleepwalking, 126; in studies of angina attacks, 125; in studying sleep deprivation, 106-107, 111; modern use of, 56-64, 66-68; spindle patterns on, 152-153; when sleep ration cut in half, 112

"elektroson," 127-128

elephants, sleeping habits of, 36

endocrine glands, 143, 144

ESP (extrasensory perception), 93-94

estivation, 145-146

evolution of sleep, in animal kingdom, 46

exercise, in relation to sleep patterns, 130-131
eyes closed while asleep, 35

fear center, 96
Feinberg, Irwin, 93
fiddler crabs, 25
filefish, sleeping posture and night color of, 37
films, relation of, to dreams, 92
fish, sleeping positions of, 36-37
Fisher, Charles, 83, 153
Foulkes, David, and Rechtschaffen, Allan, 92
free association, in interpreting dreams, 75, 82
Freud, Sigmund, 73-75, 89, 90
frogs, hibernation of, 136

ground squirrel: as prey animal, 39-40; golden-mantled, hibernation of, 142; in estivation, 146
grunions, 24. See also mating cycles
guinea pig: adaptability of, to sleeping in laboratory, 39; as prey animal, 40; mating behavior of, 28; newborn, 44

Halberg, Franz, 32
Hall, Calvin, "dream catalog," 90-91
hallucinations, during sleep deprivation, 107-108, 110
hamster: heartbeat of, 142; hibernation of, 141
heart: during REM sleep, 66; during sleep, 13; in relation to circadian rhythms, 22
hedgehog, hibernation of, 141
hemispheres of brain, 96, 97
Hernandez-Peon, Raul, 100, 104
Hess, Walter, 98
hibernation: arousal from, 140-141; in laboratory, 142
hippocampus, electrodes in, 40, 41

homeotherms, 137; migration of, 137, 144
hoofed animals: adaptability of, to sleeping in laboratory, 39; as prey animals, 40; young of, 44
human menstrual cycle, 25; relation of, to dreams, 91
hunger center, 96
Huxley, Julian, 34-35
"hypnotoxins," 103
hypothalamus: control regions in, 96, 152-153; effect of acetylcholine on, 100-101; effect of adrenalin on, 101; sleep control centers in, 98; stimulation of, in REM sleep, 91-92

infants: paradoxical sleep in, 44; REM sleep in, 87-88; sleep patterns of, 16; sleep requirements of, 14
inner clocks, 22, 26, 28, 29, 32
insects, hibernation of, 135-136
insomnia, 103, 116, 117-123; drugs for relief of, 118; effects of, 118; electric sleep therapy for, 127-128; equipment for relief of, 118; worry of losing sleep and, 132
Interpretation of Dreams, The, by Sigmund Freud, 74
invertebrates, 50

jet exhaustion, 29-31
Joseph, ancient dream interpreter, 71-72
Jouvet, Michel, 101, 114, 115
Jung, Carl, 75-76

Kales, Anthony, 122, 123
Kamiya, Joe, 151
kidneys, in relation to circadian rhythms, 22
Kleitman, Dr. Nathaniel, 16, 22, 76-79
Kline, Nathan, 103

"larks" ("early people"), 21, 130
Librium, 123
lifespan: of bats, 52; of shrew, 52
limiting sleep, effects of, on waking life, 112-113
locus coeruleus, 101
lungfish, as estivators, 146

macaques: as strong fighters, 39; sleep habits of, in laboratory, 38-39
marine worms, 24-25. *See also* mating cycles
marmot, hibernation of, 141-142
marsupials, 49-50
mating cycles: of grunions, 24; of marine worms, 24-25
medulla, 96
"memory bank," 82
metabolism, in shrew and bat, 52
mice, effect of X-rays on, 31-32
migration, seasonal mechanisms controlling, 25
military, effects of sleep deprivation on, 111
milk, effect of, on sleep, 129, 131-132
Miller, Neal, 152
moles: as predators, 39; laboratory studies of sleep of, 39; sleeping habits of, 50
monkeys: dreaming of, 45-46; experiments on brain electricity in, 56
monoamine oxidase inhibitors, 101-102, 118; as "psychic energizers," 103, 118; side effects of, 103
monoamine oxidases, 101
monoamines, 101
moon, 24, 25
motor zones, 98
myoclonic jerk, 61, 62

naps, 14; catnaps, 43; "microsleep," 106, 110, 111
nightmares: during withdrawal of

sleeping pills, 122-123; recurrent, 83
nocturnal creatures, 20-21
noradrenalin, 101, 116

Oswald, Ian, 86, 108, 121, 122, 123, 124
owl, sleep and hunt cycle of, 34
"owls" ("late people"), 21, 130
oxygen, reduction of need for, during hibernation, 136, 142
oysters, feeding of, in relation to tides, 27-28

pancreas, relation of, to hibernation, 143
paradoxical sleep, 42-43, 50; appearance of animal during, 46; in echidnas and moles, 50; in egg-laying animals, 49; monkeys in, 45; stage associated with dreaming, 44. *See also* REM sleep
peas, 20
photosynthesis, 20
Pittendrigh, Colin S., 25
pituitary gland, during hibernation, 143
placebo, 120
pleasure center, 96
poikilotherms, 134, 135, 136, 140, 147
pons, 96
porgy, color change of, 37
potato tuber, "breathing" rate of, 28-29
predators, 20-21
primitive beliefs about sleep, 13, 95-96
progesterone, 124-125
psychoanalyst, 75, 76

rabbit: adaptability of, to sleeping in laboratory, 39; as prey animal, 40; napping habits of, 34; sleep experiments on, 56

RAS (reticular activating system), 99-
100; in relation to heavy meal before bedtime, 132; in relation to
worry, 132; interaction of, with
raphe system and locus coeruleus,
101
rats: effect of tryptophan on, 124;
influence of sodium pentobarbital
on, 31; in hibernation experiments,
144; injections of cerebrospinal
fluid into, 103-104
"REM rebound," 112, 115; after withdrawal of barbiturates, 122
REM sleep (rapid eye movements), 42,
44, 76-78, 79, 81, 82, 83-85, 86;
ability of volunteers to distinguish,
153; after bed-wetting, 126; deprivation of, 113, 114, 115; effect
of amphetamines on, 123, 125;
effect of barbiturates on, 121-122;
effect of tryptophan on, 124; elimi-
nation of, by monoamine oxidase
inhibitor, 102; hypotheses on function of, 93; in infants, 87-88; in
short sleep periods, 130; in sleep
cycle, 66-67; mental excitement of,
125; personality changes after deprivation of, 114; produced by
locus coeruleus, 101; reduction of,
after period of sleep deprivation,
111; stimulation of hypothalamus
and, 91-92. See also paradoxical
sleep
reptiles: cold-blooded, 134; not true
sleepers, 48
respirometer, 28-29
robin, sleeping position of, 34

satiety center, 96
senses: alertness of, while sleeping,
14; before and after birth, 43;
while trying to sleep, 132
sensory zones, 98
"sentinel" mechanism, 42

serotonin, 101-102, 124
shrew: habits of, 52; lifespan of, in
comparison to bat, 52
sleep: amount of, 14, 130; amount of,
at different ages, 93; attitudes
toward, 14-15; effect of monoamine
oxidase inhibitors on, 102-103;
quality of, 151; ration of, cut in
half, 112
sleep control center, 98
sleep deprivation: effects of, 16, 107-
113; partial, 111-112
sleep learning, 148-151
sleepiness during pregnancy, 124
sleeping pills, 118-125
sleeping sickness, 98
sleepwalking, 14, 84, 125-126
"slow-wave sleep," 52; during sleep
deprivation, 107; energy-saving
function of, 52; in birds in laboratory, 48, 52; in cats, 41-42; in
echidnas, 50; in egg-laying mammals, 50; in opossums, 49; in sleepwalking, 126; not affected by monoamine oxidase inhibitors, 102; produced by serotonin, 101; relationship of, to paradoxical sleep, 46
snails: hibernation of, 136; tropical,
estivation of, 146-147
snake, ringed, sleep and hunt cycle
of, 34
snakes, hibernation of, 136
snoring, 14, 33
Snyder, Frederic, 42
sodium pentobarbital, effect on animals of, 31
speech-association zones, 98
spinal cord, 96
stage 1 sleep, 63, 78
stage 2 sleep, 63, 78, 153
stage 3 sleep, 63-64, 82-83
stage 4 sleep, 64, 66, 67, 78, 82-83;
bed-wetting in, 84, 126-127; deprivation of, 115-116; effect of

Dalmane on, 123; nightmares in, 83, 125; sleepwalking in, 84, 125-126; when sleep ration cut in half, 112
swallowing center, 96
swifts, sleeping habits of, 48

thirst center, 96
Thomas, Lowell, 29-30
thyroid, possible relation to hibernation of, 143
time zone, 22, 29-30, 31
toads, hibernation of, 136
tranquilizers, 118
Tripp, Peter, 106-108
tryptophan, 124; in milk, 131-132
twenty-eight hour day, in human experiments, 22, 23
twenty-one hour day, in human experiments, 22, 23

Valium, 123
Van Twyver, Henry, 39, 46, 48, 49, 50, 52
Verrill, A. E., 36-37
von Frisch, Karl, 26-27

"waggle dance," 26
"walkathons," 106
Webb, Wilse, 115
Weitnauer, E., 48
Wendt, C. F., 144
Wilkinson, R. T., 112-113
Wolpert, Edward, incorporating experiences into dreams, 90
woodchuck: hibernation of, 139-140, 141, 142; mating of, 141
work schedules: human adaptability to, 22; U.S. Navy and Air Force experiments on, 32

Young, W. C., 28

About the Authors

ALVIN SILVERSTEIN, born in New York City and raised in Brooklyn, developed an early interest in science. He received his B.A. from Brooklyn College, his M.A. from the University of Pennsylvania, and his Ph.D. from New York University. He is Professor of Biology at the Staten Island Community College of City University of New York.

VIRGINIA SILVERSTEIN grew up in Philadelphia and received her B.A. from the University of Pennsylvania. After her marriage, she worked as a free-lance translator of Russian scientific literature, doing extensive work for government and private agencies.

The Silversteins, who have collaborated on over thirty science books for young readers, live on a farm near Lebanon, New Jersey, with their six children.